A TOUCH
OF
EXCELLENCE

A Comprehensive Guide to Personal and Professional Growth

Perry Jackson

**Copyright © 2024 by Perry Jackson
All Rights Reserved**

No part of this book may be used or reproduced by any means, whether graphic, electronic, or mechanical, including photocopying, recording, taping, or by any information storage or retrieval system without the written permission of the publisher.

A TOUCH OF EXCELLENCE

TABLE OF CONTENTS

INTRODUCTION

Part I
Understanding the Landscape of Excellence

CHAPTER 1
Demystifying Excellence: Separating Myth from Reality
Traditional Views of Excellence
The Hero's Journey
The All-or-Nothing Mentality

CHAPTER 2
Unveiling the Competition: A Strategic Analysis
Strengths, Weaknesses, and Opportunities: A Competitive Landscape Analysis
Competitive Landscape Analysis

CHAPTER 3
The Power of Differentiation: Carving Your Unique Niche
Highlighting What Sets You Apart

Part II
Cultivating the Habits and Mindsets of Excellence

CHAPTER 4
The Power of Purpose: Aligning Your Goals with Excellence
Setting SMART Goals for Continuous Improvement

CHAPTER 5
Embracing a Growth Mindset: Fostering a Love for Learning
Developing Effective Learning Strategies

CHAPTER 6
Building Resilience: Overcoming Obstacles on the Path to Excellence
Developing Strategies for Overcoming Challenges

Part III
Mastering the Art of Excellence In Action

CHAPTER 7
Crafting a Personalized Action Plan: Putting Theory into Practice
Developing Actionable Steps and Milestones

CHAPTER 8
Cultivating Effective Habits: The Building Blocks of Excellence
Strategies for Habit Formation and Consistency

CHAPTER 9

Mastering Time Management: Optimising Your Workflow for Excellence

Creating a Sustainable Work-Life Balance

Part IV

Amplifying Your Excellence: Strategies for Visibility and Impact

CHAPTER 10

The Power of Storytelling: Sharing Your Journey and Inspiring Others

Leveraging Storytelling for Personal Branding

CHAPTER 11

Building a Strong Online Presence: Connecting with Your Audience

Content Marketing Strategies for Audience Engagement

Understanding Audience Engagemen

CHAPTER 12

Building a Community of Excellence: Collaboration and Support

Fostering a Supportive Network for Continuous Growth

CONCLUSION

Appendix

Index

INTRODUCTION

The pursuit of excellence is a universal human aspiration, a relentless drive to surpass limitations and achieve extraordinary results. Yet, the concept of excellence is as multifaceted as the individuals who strive for it. What does it truly mean to excel? Is it measured solely by tangible achievements, or does it encompass intangible qualities like character, compassion, and wisdom?

To embark on a meaningful journey towards excellence, we must first clarify our own definition of the term. Excellence is not a static state; it's a dynamic process of continuous growth and improvement. It's about pushing the boundaries of our potential, not just meeting expectations. It's about aligning our actions with our values, and finding fulfilment in the journey, rather than solely the destination.

In the realm of professional life, excellence might be synonymous with innovation, leadership, and delivering exceptional results. In the realm of personal growth, it could be about cultivating inner peace, building strong relationships, and contributing positively to society. For athletes, excellence is often equated with physical prowess, mental fortitude, and unwavering dedication.

Ultimately, the definition of excellence is unique to each individual. It's a personal compass that guides our choices, motivates our actions, and shapes our identity. To achieve true excellence, we must delve deep within ourselves to uncover our passions, strengths, and values. Only then can we set meaningful goals and embark on a path of purposeful growth.

Identifying Your Target Audience
Understanding your target audience is crucial for delivering a message that resonates. Who are you writing for? Are you addressing aspiring entrepreneurs, seasoned professionals, or

individuals seeking personal growth? Perhaps you're targeting a specific industry or niche.

By clearly defining your target audience, you can tailor your content to their specific needs, challenges, and aspirations. This will enable you to create a more impactful and relevant book that connects with readers on a deeper level.

Consider creating detailed reader personas to help you visualise your ideal reader. What are their demographics, interests, and goals? What challenges do they face? What are their hopes and dreams? By understanding your target audience intimately, you can craft a message that speaks directly to their hearts and minds.

Part I

Understanding the Landscape of Excellence

Chapter 1

Demystifying Excellence: Separating Myth from Reality

The pursuit of excellence has been a cornerstone of human civilization for millennia. From the ancient Greek ideal of arete to the Renaissance concept of virtu, societies have long held up certain individuals as exemplars of human achievement. These figures, whether they were philosophers, artists, or warriors, were often placed on pedestals, their accomplishments seen as unattainable for ordinary mortals.

This reverence for exceptional individuals has contributed to a pervasive myth about excellence: that it is an inherent quality possessed by a select few, a divine gift bestowed upon the lucky or the chosen. This myth reinforces the belief that excellence is a distant, unattainable ideal, reserved for geniuses and prodigies. It can foster feelings of inadequacy and discourage individuals from even attempting to strive for greatness.

Another common misconception is that excellence is solely defined by external achievements. This perspective equates success with material possessions, titles, or accolades.

While these markers can certainly be indicators of achievement, they do not encapsulate the full essence of excellence. True excellence is a multifaceted concept that encompasses not only external accomplishments but also internal qualities such as character, integrity, and wisdom.

Furthermore, the traditional view of excellence often implies a solitary pursuit. The image of the lone genius, toiling away in isolation, has become a powerful archetype in our culture. However, this narrative overlooks the importance of collaboration, mentorship, and support systems in achieving greatness. True excellence is often the product of collective effort and shared knowledge.

It is essential to challenge these traditional views of excellence and replace them with a more inclusive and attainable perspective. By demystifying the concept of excellence, we can empower individuals to recognize their own potential and embark on their own journeys of growth and achievement.

In the following sections, we will explore the various facets of excellence, debunking common myths and replacing them with evidence-based insights. We will examine the role of mindset, habits, and environment in cultivating excellence. We will also discuss the importance of balance, resilience, and lifelong learning in sustaining a pursuit of excellence.

Traditional Views of Excellence

The Cult of Genius
One of the most persistent myths surrounding excellence is the cult of genius. This notion

posits that extraordinary achievements are the sole province of a select few individuals blessed with innate talent and brilliance. The idea is that these geniuses are born, not made, and possess a unique cognitive capacity that sets them apart from the rest of humanity.

This perspective has deep roots in Western thought, dating back to the ancient Greeks who believed in a divine spark that ignited the minds of exceptional individuals. The Romantic era, with its emphasis on individual creativity and inspiration, further solidified the image of the solitary genius as a cultural icon.

The cult of genius has had a profound impact on our collective psyche. It can create a sense of awe and admiration for those deemed exceptional, but it can also foster feelings of inadequacy and inferiority in those who do not perceive themselves as geniuses. This belief can stifle ambition and prevent individuals from reaching their full potential.

However, a growing body of research challenges the notion of innate genius. Studies in psychology, neuroscience, and education have shown that while talent plays a role in success, it is far from being the sole determinant. Deliberate practice, perseverance, and a growth mindset are equally, if not more important factors in achieving excellence.

While it is undeniable that some individuals possess extraordinary abilities, it is equally important to recognize that these abilities are often developed through years of dedicated practice and hard work. The myth of the innate genius can obscure the reality that excellence is attainable for anyone who is willing to put in the necessary effort.

The Hero's Journey

Another prevalent myth surrounding excellence is the hero's journey narrative. This archetypal story follows a protagonist who embarks on a perilous quest, faces numerous challenges, and ultimately triumphs over adversity. The hero's journey has been a powerful storytelling device throughout history, inspiring countless works of literature, film, and art.

While the hero's journey can be a compelling narrative, it can also create unrealistic expectations about the path to excellence. It often portrays success as a solitary endeavour, achieved through dramatic feats of courage and willpower. This perspective can downplay the importance of support systems, mentors, and collaboration in achieving greatness.

Moreover, the hero's journey often implies a linear progression towards a final, definitive goal. In reality, the path to excellence is rarely straightforward. It is characterised by setbacks, failures, and periods of doubt. The journey itself is often more rewarding than the destination.

It is essential to recognize that the hero's journey is just one possible narrative of success. There are countless other paths to excellence, each with its own unique challenges and rewards. By embracing a more nuanced understanding of the journey, we can develop a more realistic and sustainable approach to achieving our goals.

The All-or-Nothing Mentality

The pursuit of excellence can sometimes be accompanied by an all-or-nothing mentality. This mindset suggests that one must achieve perfection in every aspect of their life in order to be considered successful. This pressure to be flawless can lead to burnout, anxiety, and a fear of failure.

The all-or-nothing mentality is often fueled by unrealistic expectations and societal pressures. It can be particularly prevalent in competitive environments, where individuals feel compelled to outperform their peers at all costs.

However, it is important to recognize that perfection is an unattainable ideal. Mistakes, setbacks, and failures are inevitable parts of the human experience. Embracing imperfection can actually be liberating, as it allows us to focus on progress rather than outcome.

A more balanced approach to excellence involves setting realistic goals, celebrating small wins, and learning from setbacks. It is about striving for continuous improvement rather than achieving a static state of perfection. By adopting a growth mindset, we can embrace challenges as opportunities for growth and development.

The Sole Focus on Outcomes

A common misconception about excellence is that it is solely defined by outcomes or results. This perspective can lead to a narrow focus on achieving specific goals, without considering the process or the impact of one's actions on others.

While outcomes are undoubtedly important, they should not be the sole measure of excellence. The journey towards a goal is often as valuable as the destination itself. The skills, knowledge, and relationships developed along the way can be equally, if not more, important than the final result.

Moreover, a sole focus on outcomes can lead to unethical behaviour and a disregard for the well-being of others. It is essential to balance the pursuit of personal excellence with a commitment to social responsibility and ethical conduct.

By shifting our focus from outcomes to the process, we can cultivate a more holistic and sustainable approach to excellence. This involves paying attention to our mindset, habits, and relationships, as well as the impact of our actions on others.

Chapter 2

Unveiling the Competition: A Strategic Analysis

Identifying Your Top Competitors

The strength of any business strategy lies not only in its understanding of its own strengths and weaknesses but also in its ability to recognize the competitive landscape in which it operates. This chapter aims to guide you through the crucial process of identifying and analysing your competitors, laying the foundation for a robust and informed strategy.

1. Identifying Your Top Competitors

The first step in competitor analysis is identifying who your competitors truly are. While this might seem straightforward at first glance, it requires a nuanced understanding of your market and your target audience.

1.1 Direct vs. Indirect Competitors

- **Direct Competitors:** These are businesses that offer the same or similar products or services to the same target audience. For example, Coca-Cola and Pepsi are direct competitors in the soft drink market.
- **Indirect Competitors:** These are businesses that offer different products or services but fulfil the same customer need or want. For instance, a fast-food restaurant and a grocery store might be indirect competitors as they both offer food options, although in different formats.

1.2 Identifying Direct Competitors

Identifying direct competitors can be done through various methods:

- **Market Research:** Conducting market research will help you identify the major players in your industry and their market share. This information is often available through industry reports, market analysis, and competitor websites.
- **Customer Surveys:** Asking your customers about their buying habits and

alternative choices can reveal their awareness of your competitors and their perception of their offerings.
- **Online Search:** Conducting online searches using keywords related to your business can identify companies that appear in search results alongside your own.
- **Social Media Monitoring:** Observing conversations and interactions on social media platforms can highlight brands that are frequently mentioned alongside your own or are engaging with the same audience.

1.3 Identifying Indirect Competitors

Identifying indirect competitors requires a deeper understanding of your customers' needs and wants. It involves looking beyond the obvious products or services and considering alternative ways in which customers can fulfil those needs.

- **Customer Needs Analysis:** Conduct a thorough analysis of your customers' needs and the underlying motivations behind their purchase decisions. This will

help you identify alternative products or services that can satisfy the same needs.
- **Substitute Products:** Consider products or services that offer a different solution to the same problem. For example, a taxi service and a ride-sharing app are substitute products as they both offer transportation solutions.
- **Complementary Products:** Think about products or services that are often used or purchased in conjunction with your own. These products or services can indirectly compete with yours if they offer a bundled solution that fulfils the same customer need.

1.4 The Importance of Identifying Both Direct and Indirect Competitors

It's important to identify both direct and indirect competitors because they both pose a threat to your business, although in different ways.

- **Direct competitors** compete for the same market share and customer base. They are a direct threat to your sales and revenue.
- **Indirect competitors** compete for the same customer need or want. They are a

threat to your market share and can influence customer choices in the long run.

Understanding both types of competitors is essential for developing a comprehensive strategy that addresses the entire competitive landscape. It allows you to anticipate potential threats, identify opportunities for differentiation, and develop strategies to stay ahead of the curve.

Analysing Your Competitors

Once you have identified your top competitors, the next step is to conduct a thorough analysis of their strategies, strengths, and weaknesses. This will provide you with valuable insights into their competitive advantages and potential vulnerabilities, informing your own strategic decisions.

2.1 Competitive Intelligence Gathering

Competitive intelligence gathering involves collecting and analysing information about your competitors from various sources. This information can include:

- **Company Websites and Marketing Materials:** These provide insights into their products or services, target audience, pricing strategies, and marketing messages.
- **Financial Reports and Investor Presentations:** These offer information about their financial performance, growth plans, and investment priorities.
- **Industry Reports and Market Analysis:** These provide an overview of the competitive landscape, market trends, and industry forecasts.
- **Customer Reviews and Social Media Interactions:** These offer insights into customer perceptions of their products or services, their strengths and weaknesses, and their customer service.
- **Employee Reviews and Job Postings:** These can reveal information about their company culture, employee satisfaction, and talent acquisition strategies.

2.2 SWOT Analysis

A SWOT analysis is a framework for evaluating a company's strengths, weaknesses, opportunities, and threats. It is a valuable tool for competitor analysis as it helps you identify their competitive advantages and potential vulnerabilities.

- **Strengths:** Identify your competitors' internal capabilities and resources that give them a competitive edge. This can include their brand reputation, product quality, technological innovation, distribution network, or customer service.
- **Weaknesses:** Identify your competitors' internal limitations or vulnerabilities that can be exploited. This can include their high prices, limited product range, poor customer service, or outdated technology.
- **Opportunities:** Identify external factors that can be leveraged to your competitors' advantage. This can include emerging market trends, new technologies, or changes in regulations.
- **Threats:** Identify external factors that can pose a risk to your competitors' business. This can include economic downturns, new entrants into the market, or disruptive technologies.

2.3 Competitive Positioning

Competitive positioning refers to how a company differentiates itself from its competitors in the minds of its target customers. It involves identifying your unique value proposition and communicating it effectively to your audience.

- **Value Proposition:** Identify what makes your products or services unique and valuable to your customers. This can include your product features, pricing, customer service, or brand experience.
- **Target Audience:** Identify your ideal customers and their specific needs and wants. This will help you tailor your messaging and offerings to resonate with them.
- **Positioning Strategy:** Develop a clear and concise message that communicates your unique value proposition to your target audience. This message should be consistent across all your marketing channels and touchpoints.

2.4 Benchmarking

Benchmarking involves comparing your company's performance against that of your competitors on key metrics. This can include metrics such as sales, profitability, customer satisfaction, or employee engagement.

- **Key Performance Indicators (KPIs):** Identify the most important metrics for your business and track them regularly.
- **Competitor Data:** Gather data on your competitors' performance on the same KPIs. This information can be obtained from various sources, such as financial reports, industry benchmarks, or customer surveys.
- **Performance Gap Analysis:** Compare your performance against that of your competitors and identify areas where you are lagging behind. This will help you identify areas for improvement and develop strategies to close the gap.

Developing a Competitive Strategy

Once you have a thorough understanding of your competitors, the final step is to develop a competitive strategy that leverages your strengths, addresses your weaknesses, and positions you for success in the marketplace.

3.1 Cost Leadership

A cost leadership strategy involves offering products or services at a lower cost than your competitors. This can be achieved through various means, such as economies of scale, efficient operations, or low-cost sourcing.

- **Advantages:** Cost leadership can attract price-sensitive customers and increase market share.
- **Challenges:** Maintaining low costs can be difficult in the long run, and it can lead to a perception of lower quality.

3.2 Differentiation

A differentiation strategy involves offering unique and valuable products or services that distinguish you from your competitors. This can be achieved through product innovation, superior customer service, or a strong brand identity.

- **Advantages:** Differentiation can command premium prices and create customer loyalty.
- **Challenges:** Differentiation can be difficult to maintain in the long run, and it can be imitated by competitors.

3.3 Focus

A focus strategy involves targeting a specific niche market segment and tailoring your products or services to their specific needs and wants. This can be achieved through specialised expertise, personalised service, or a unique product offering.

- **Advantages:** Focus can create a strong competitive advantage in a specific market segment.
- **Challenges:** Focus can limit your growth potential and make you vulnerable to changes in the market.

3.4 Hybrid Strategies

Many companies adopt a hybrid strategy that combines elements of cost leadership, differentiation, and focus. This allows them to leverage their strengths and address their weaknesses in a more flexible and adaptive way.

- **Advantages:** Hybrid strategies can offer the benefits of multiple strategies while mitigating their risks.

- **Challenges:** Hybrid strategies can be complex to implement and require careful balancing of different objectives.

3.5 Ongoing Monitoring and Adaptation

The competitive landscape is constantly evolving, so it's important to monitor your competitors' activities and adapt your strategy accordingly. This involves staying informed about their new products or services, pricing changes, marketing campaigns, and strategic moves.

- **Competitive Intelligence:** Continue to gather and analyse information about your competitors on an ongoing basis.
- **Strategic Agility:** Be prepared to adjust your strategy in response to changes in the market or your competitors' actions.
- **Innovation:** Continuously innovate and improve your products or services to stay ahead of the curve.

Note: Competitor analysis is a critical component of any successful business strategy. It provides you with the insights you need to understand your competitive landscape, identify your strengths and weaknesses, and develop a strategy that positions you for success. By identifying your top competitors, analysing their strategies, and developing a competitive strategy of your own, you can gain a competitive edge and achieve your business goals.

Remember, competitor analysis is not a one-time event. It is an ongoing process that requires constant monitoring and adaptation. By staying informed about your competitors' activities and adapting your strategy accordingly, you can stay ahead of the curve and thrive in the ever-changing marketplace.

Additional Notes:

- The word count for each section may vary slightly depending on the specific industry and the depth of analysis required.
- The information provided in this chapter is a general overview of competitor analysis. It is important to tailor your approach to the specific needs and circumstances of your business.
- Competitor analysis is an ongoing process. It is important to continue to

monitor your competitors' activities and adapt your strategy accordingly.

Strengths, Weaknesses, and Opportunities: A Competitive Landscape Analysis

In the dynamic and ever-evolving business world, understanding the strengths, weaknesses, and opportunities present in your competitive landscape is paramount. This analysis provides a comprehensive overview of the key players, their strategies, and the external factors that shape the market. By conducting a thorough SWOT (Strengths, Weaknesses, Opportunities, and Threats) analysis of your competitors and the broader market, you can gain valuable insights to inform your strategic decision-making and position your business for success.

Strengths:

- **Strong Brand Recognition and Reputation:** Established players often benefit from strong brand recognition and

a positive reputation built over time. This can lead to increased customer loyalty, trust, and a competitive advantage in attracting new customers.
- **Extensive Distribution Network:** A well-established distribution network can provide a significant advantage by ensuring wider product availability and accessibility for customers. This can be particularly crucial in industries where physical presence and reach are essential.
- **Economies of Scale:** Larger companies often enjoy economies of scale, allowing them to produce goods or services at a lower cost per unit. This cost advantage can translate into lower prices for customers or higher profit margins for the company.
- **Technological Innovation and R&D Capabilities:** Companies that invest heavily in research and development (R&D) can gain a competitive edge by developing innovative products or processes that differentiate them from their rivals. This can lead to increased market share, higher prices, and improved profitability.

- **Skilled and Experienced Workforce:** A talented and experienced workforce can be a significant asset, contributing to higher productivity, innovation, and customer satisfaction. Companies with a strong employer brand and a positive work culture can attract and retain top talent, further enhancing their competitive advantage.
- **Financial Strength and Resources:** Access to capital and financial resources can enable companies to invest in growth initiatives, pursue acquisitions, and weather economic downturns. This financial stability can provide a significant advantage in competitive markets.
- **Effective Marketing and Advertising Strategies:** Companies with well-developed marketing and advertising strategies can effectively reach their target audience, build brand awareness, and influence consumer behaviour. This can lead to increased sales and market share.
- **Strong Customer Relationships and Loyalty:** Building and maintaining strong customer relationships can lead to repeat business, positive word-of-mouth

recommendations, and a competitive advantage in attracting new customers.
- **Strategic Partnerships and Alliances:** Collaborating with other companies can provide access to new markets, technologies, or resources, leading to increased growth opportunities and a stronger competitive position.

Weaknesses:

- **High Costs and Inefficiencies:** Some companies may struggle with high operating costs, outdated processes, or inefficient supply chains. These weaknesses can lead to lower profit margins, higher prices for customers, and a competitive disadvantage.
- **Limited Product or Service Offerings:** Companies with a narrow product or service portfolio may be vulnerable to changes in consumer preferences or the emergence of new competitors offering a wider range of options.
- **Weak Brand Image or Reputation:** Companies with a negative brand image or reputation may struggle to attract and

retain customers, leading to lower sales and market share.
- **Lack of Innovation:** Companies that fail to invest in innovation and R&D may fall behind their competitors in terms of product development and process improvement. This can lead to a loss of market share and reduced profitability.
- **Inadequate Customer Service:** Poor customer service can damage a company's reputation and lead to customer dissatisfaction and churn. Companies that fail to prioritise customer experience may struggle to compete in markets where service is a key differentiator.
- **Limited Distribution Network:** Companies with a limited distribution network may struggle to reach their target audience, leading to lower sales and missed opportunities.
- **Financial Constraints:** Companies with limited access to capital or financial resources may struggle to invest in growth initiatives, pursue acquisitions, or weather economic downturns. This financial vulnerability can be a significant weakness in competitive markets.

- **Ineffective Marketing and Advertising:** Companies with poorly executed marketing and advertising strategies may struggle to reach their target audience, build brand awareness, or influence consumer behaviour. This can lead to lower sales and market share.
- **Internal Conflicts and Inefficiencies:** Internal conflicts, poor communication, or inefficient decision-making processes can hinder a company's ability to respond effectively to market changes or competitive threats.

Opportunities:

- **Emerging Markets and New Customer Segments:** Expanding into new markets or targeting underserved customer segments can provide significant growth opportunities for companies. This may involve adapting products or services to meet the specific needs of these new markets or developing innovative solutions to address unmet needs.
- **Technological Advancements:** New technologies can create opportunities for companies to improve their products,

processes, or services, leading to increased efficiency, innovation, and competitive advantage. Companies that embrace and leverage new technologies can gain a significant edge in the market.

- **Changes in Consumer Preferences and Behavior:** Shifting consumer preferences and behaviours can create opportunities for companies that are able to adapt their offerings to meet these changing needs. This may involve developing new products or services, modifying existing ones, or adopting new marketing and communication strategies.
- **Economic Growth and Increased Consumer Spending:** Periods of economic growth and increased consumer spending can provide opportunities for companies to expand their market share and increase sales. Companies that are well-positioned to capitalise on these favourable economic conditions can experience significant growth.
- **Strategic Partnerships and Alliances:** Collaborating with other companies can provide access to new markets, technologies, or resources, leading to increased growth opportunities and a

stronger competitive position. Strategic partnerships can enable companies to leverage each other's strengths and achieve mutually beneficial outcomes.
- **Regulatory Changes:** Changes in regulations or government policies can create opportunities for companies that are able to adapt their operations or offerings to comply with the new requirements. This may involve developing new products or services, modifying existing ones, or adopting new business practices.
- **Mergers and Acquisitions:** Acquiring or merging with other companies can provide access to new markets, technologies, or resources, leading to increased growth opportunities and a stronger competitive position. This can be a particularly effective strategy in industries where consolidation is occurring or where there are opportunities to leverage synergies between companies.

Threats:

- **Intense Competition:** High levels of competition can lead to price wars, reduced profit margins, and a constant

need to innovate and differentiate. Companies operating in highly competitive markets must be agile and adaptable to stay ahead.
- **Economic Downturns:** Economic recessions or downturns can lead to reduced consumer spending, lower sales, and increased financial pressure for companies. Companies that are not well-prepared to weather economic downturns may struggle to survive.
- **Technological Disruptions:** New technologies can disrupt entire industries, rendering existing products or services obsolete. Companies that fail to adapt to technological changes may face significant challenges and even extinction.
- **Changes in Consumer Preferences and Behavior:** Shifting consumer preferences and behaviours can pose a threat to companies that are unable or unwilling to adapt their offerings to meet these changing needs.
- **Regulatory Changes:** Changes in regulations or government policies can create challenges for companies that are not prepared to comply with the new requirements. This may involve

significant investments in new technologies, processes, or business practices.
- **New Entrants into the Market:** The emergence of new competitors can disrupt the market, intensify competition, and put pressure on existing players. Companies must be vigilant in monitoring new entrants and adapting their strategies to maintain their competitive position.
- **Supply Chain Disruptions:** disruptions in the supply chain, such as natural disasters, political instability, or pandemics, can impact a company's ability to produce or deliver its products or services. This can lead to lost sales, customer dissatisfaction, and financial losses.
- **Global Events and Geopolitical Risks:** Global events such as wars, terrorist attacks, or pandemics can create uncertainty and instability in the market, impacting consumer confidence and business operations. Companies must be prepared to manage these risks and adapt their strategies accordingly.

Competitive Landscape Analysis:

A competitive landscape analysis involves evaluating the strengths, weaknesses, opportunities, and threats of your competitors and the broader market. This analysis can help you identify your competitive advantages, potential vulnerabilities, and areas for improvement. It can also help you develop a more informed and effective business strategy.

By understanding the strengths, weaknesses, and opportunities present in your competitive landscape, you can make more informed strategic decisions, identify potential threats, and capitalise on emerging opportunities. This knowledge can help you position your business for success in a dynamic and ever-changing market.

CHAPTER 3

The Power of Differentiation: Carving Your Unique Niche

Developing a Compelling Unique Selling Proposition (USP)

In today's crowded and competitive marketplace, standing out from the crowd is essential for any business seeking to thrive. Differentiation is the key to achieving this, and at its core lies the development of a compelling Unique Selling Proposition (USP). This chapter will delve into the concept of differentiation, explore the process of creating a strong USP, and illustrate how it can be leveraged to carve out a unique niche and achieve sustainable success.

Developing a Compelling Unique Selling Proposition (USP)

A Unique Selling Proposition (USP) is a statement that clearly and concisely articulates the unique benefits and value that a product or service offers to its customers. It is the essence of what sets your business apart from the competition and answers the crucial question: "Why should customers choose you?" A strong USP is not merely a marketing slogan; it is a strategic foundation that guides all aspects of your business, from product development to customer service.

Understanding the Importance of a USP

In a world where consumers are bombarded with countless choices, a compelling USP acts as a beacon, guiding them towards your brand. It provides clarity and focus, making it easier for customers to understand what you offer and why they should choose you over the competition. A strong USP can:

- **Attract and retain customers:** By clearly articulating the unique value you offer, a USP can attract customers who are seeking those specific benefits. It can also foster customer loyalty by reinforcing their decision to choose your brand.
- **Differentiate your brand:** A USP sets you apart from the competition, highlighting what makes you unique and valuable. This differentiation can help you command premium prices, increase

market share, and build a strong brand identity.
- **Guide marketing and communication efforts:** A USP provides a clear and concise message that can be used across all marketing and communication channels. This consistency strengthens your brand image and reinforces your value proposition.
- **Drive innovation and product development:** A USP can inspire innovation by focusing your efforts on developing products or services that deliver on your unique value proposition.
- **Enhance employee engagement:** A clear USP can help employees understand the company's mission and values, fostering a sense of purpose and pride in their work.

Identifying Your Unique Strengths and Value

The first step in developing a compelling USP is to identify your unique strengths and the value you offer to your customers. This involves a deep understanding of your business, your target audience, and your competitive landscape. Consider the following questions:

- **What are you good at?** Identify your core competencies, skills, and resources that set you apart from the competition. This could be your expertise in a particular field, your innovative technology, your superior customer service, or your unique brand story.
- **What do your customers value?** Understand your target audience's needs, wants, and pain points. What are they looking for in a product or service? What problems do they need to solve? What benefits do they value most?
- **What makes you different from the competition?** Analyse your competitors' strengths and weaknesses. What do they offer? What are their gaps? How can you differentiate yourself from them?

Crafting a Clear and Compelling USP Statement

Once you have identified your unique strengths and value, it's time to craft a clear and compelling USP statement. A good USP statement should be:

- **Clear and concise:** It should be easy to understand and remember. Avoid jargon and complex language.

- **Specific and relevant:** It should focus on the specific benefits and value you offer to your target audience.
- **Unique and differentiating:** It should highlight what sets you apart from the competition.
- **Credible and believable:** It should be supported by evidence and testimonials.
- **Memorable and impactful:** It should leave a lasting impression on your audience.

Here are some examples of effective USP statements:

- **FedEx:** "When it absolutely, positively has to be there overnight."
- **Domino's Pizza:** "Hot, fresh pizza delivered in 30 minutes or less, guaranteed."
- **M&Ms:** "Melts in your mouth, not in your hand."
- **Apple:** "Think different."

Communicating Your USP Effectively

Once you have developed a compelling USP, it's crucial to communicate it effectively to your target audience. This involves integrating your

USP into all aspects of your marketing and communication efforts, including:

- **Your website and online presence:** Make sure your USP is prominently displayed on your website and social media profiles.
- **Your marketing materials:** Include your USP in your brochures, flyers, and other marketing materials.
- **Your sales pitch:** Use your USP to differentiate your products or services during sales presentations.
- **Your customer service:** Reinforce your USP through exceptional customer service that delivers on your promises.

Evolving Your USP

Your USP is not static; it should evolve as your business grows and the market changes. Regularly review your USP to ensure it remains relevant and effective. Consider the following:

- **Changes in your business:** Have your strengths or value proposition changed?
- **Changes in your target audience:** Have your customers' needs or preferences evolved?

- **Changes in the competitive landscape:** Have new competitors emerged or have existing competitors changed their strategies?

By regularly evaluating and adapting your USP, you can ensure that it continues to differentiate your brand and drive your business forward.

Developing a compelling Unique Selling Proposition is a crucial step in carving out a unique niche and achieving sustainable success in today's competitive marketplace. By understanding the importance of a USP, identifying your unique strengths and value, crafting a clear and compelling USP statement, and communicating it effectively, you can differentiate your brand, attract and retain customers, and achieve your business goals. Remember, your USP is not just a marketing slogan; it is the essence of what makes your business unique and valuable. Embrace it, nurture it, and let it guide you towards success.

Highlighting What Sets You Apart

In the dynamic and ever-evolving marketplace, where competition is fierce and consumer choices are abundant, standing out from the crowd is paramount. This chapter delves into the strategies and tactics that businesses can employ to highlight their unique qualities, effectively differentiate themselves from competitors, and carve a distinct niche in the minds of their target audience.

1. The Essence of Differentiation

Differentiation is the cornerstone of effective marketing and branding. It is the process of distinguishing your product or service from others in the market, creating a unique and compelling value proposition that resonates with your target audience. Differentiation is not merely about being different; it is about being better in a way that matters to your customers.

A strong differentiation strategy can yield numerous benefits for your business:

- **Enhanced brand recognition:** A distinct brand identity helps customers identify

and remember your business, increasing brand awareness and recall.
- **Increased customer loyalty:** When customers perceive your brand as unique and valuable, they are more likely to develop loyalty and repeat business.
- **Premium pricing:** A differentiated brand can command premium prices, as customers are willing to pay more for products or services they perceive as superior or unique.
- **Competitive advantage:** Differentiation sets you apart from the competition, making it harder for rivals to replicate your success.
- **Market leadership:** A strong differentiation strategy can position your brand as a leader in its niche, attracting a loyal customer base and influencing industry trends.

2. Identifying Your Unique Selling Points (USPs)

The first step in highlighting what sets you apart is to identify your Unique Selling Points (USPs). These are the specific attributes or benefits that make your product or service unique and valuable to your customers. USPs can be based on various factors, including:

- **Product features:** Unique product features, innovative designs, or superior quality can be powerful differentiators.
- **Price:** Offering competitive pricing, discounts, or value-added bundles can attract price-sensitive customers.
- **Customer service:** Exceptional customer service, personalised attention, or convenient support can set you apart from competitors.
- **Brand experience:** Creating a memorable and engaging brand experience, through captivating storytelling, unique visuals, or interactive marketing, can leave a lasting impression on customers.
- **Social responsibility:** Demonstrating a commitment to social or environmental causes can resonate with ethically conscious consumers.

To identify your USPs, consider the following questions:

- What are your core competencies and strengths?

- What do your customers value most?
- What problems do your products or services solve for your customers?
- What makes your brand experience unique?
- How do you differ from your competitors?

Once you have identified your USPs, it is essential to articulate them clearly and concisely in your marketing and communication efforts. This will help customers understand the unique value you offer and why they should choose your brand over others.

3. Communicating Your Differentiation

Effective communication is crucial to highlighting what sets you apart. Your marketing and communication strategies should be designed to showcase your USPs and create a clear and compelling brand message that resonates with your target audience. Consider the following tactics:

- **Develop a strong brand identity:** Your brand identity should reflect your USPs and create a consistent and memorable image across all touchpoints. This

includes your logo, colour palette, typography, and brand voice.
- **Craft a compelling brand story:** A captivating brand story can humanise your brand, connect with customers on an emotional level, and differentiate you from competitors.
- **Utilise targeted marketing:** Tailor your marketing messages and channels to reach your ideal customers and communicate your USPs effectively.
- **Leverage social media:** Social media platforms provide a powerful platform to engage with your audience, showcase your brand personality, and share your unique story.
- **Create valuable content:** Content marketing, such as blog posts, videos, and infographics, can educate and inform your audience, position your brand as a thought leader, and demonstrate your expertise.
- **Offer exceptional customer service:** Providing outstanding customer service can create a positive brand experience, foster customer loyalty, and generate positive word-of-mouth recommendations.

- **Seek media coverage and publicity:** Positive media coverage and publicity can enhance your brand reputation and credibility, reaching a wider audience and reinforcing your differentiation.

4. Reinforcing Your Differentiation

Differentiation is an ongoing process that requires constant effort and reinforcement. To maintain your competitive edge, consider the following strategies:

- **Continuously innovate:** Strive to improve your products or services, introduce new features, and stay ahead of industry trends.
- **Monitor your competition:** Keep a close eye on your competitors' strategies and tactics to ensure you maintain your differentiation.
- **Solicit customer feedback:** Regularly seek feedback from your customers to understand their needs, preferences, and perceptions of your brand.
- **Adapt to market changes:** Be prepared to adapt your differentiation strategy in response to changes in the market,

consumer behaviour, or competitive landscape.
- **Invest in your brand:** Allocate resources to marketing, branding, and customer experience initiatives to reinforce your differentiation and build a strong brand presence.

5. Examples of Successful Differentiation

Numerous brands have successfully differentiated themselves in the marketplace, achieving remarkable success and customer loyalty. Here are a few notable examples:

- **Apple:** Apple's focus on innovation, design, and user experience has created a loyal following and a premium brand image.
- **Tesla:** Tesla's commitment to sustainable energy and cutting-edge technology has disrupted the automotive industry and attracted environmentally conscious consumers.
- **Zappos:** Zappos' exceptional customer service, including free shipping and returns, has created a loyal customer base

and a reputation for exceeding expectations.
- **Warby Parker:** Warby Parker's "buy one, give one" program, combined with its stylish and affordable eyewear, has resonated with socially conscious consumers.
- **Patagonia:** Patagonia's commitment to environmental sustainability and ethical business practices has attracted outdoor enthusiasts and eco-conscious consumers.

These examples illustrate the power of differentiation in creating a unique brand identity, attracting a loyal customer base, and achieving sustainable success in a competitive marketplace.

Highlighting what sets you apart is essential for any business seeking to thrive in today's crowded marketplace. By identifying your Unique Selling Points, communicating your differentiation effectively, and reinforcing your brand message consistently, you can create a distinct and compelling brand identity that resonates with your target audience. Remember, differentiation is not a one-time event; it is an ongoing process that requires constant effort and adaptation.

By embracing innovation, monitoring your competition, and staying attuned to your customers' needs, you can maintain your competitive edge and achieve lasting success.

Part II

Cultivating the Habits and Mindsets of Excellence

CHAPTER 4

The Power of Purpose: Aligning Your Goals with Excellence

Discovering Your Core Values and Aspirations

In the pursuit of business success, it is easy to get caught up in the day-to-day operations, chasing after profits, and striving to outdo competitors. However, true and lasting success often stems from a deeper foundation - a clear sense of purpose that aligns your goals with excellence. This chapter explores the profound impact of purpose in business, guiding you through the process of discovering your core values and aspirations, and illustrating how aligning your goals with a higher purpose can lead to exceptional performance, employee engagement, and customer loyalty.

Discovering Your Core Values and Aspirations

At the heart of any purpose-driven business lies a set of core values and aspirations that define its identity and guide its actions. These values represent the fundamental beliefs and principles that shape the company's culture, decision-making, and interactions with stakeholders. Aspirations, on the other hand, embody the company's long-term vision and the positive impact it seeks to create in the world.

1. The Importance of Core Values

Core values are the guiding principles that shape a company's culture and behaviour. They define what the company stands for, how it operates, and the kind of impact it wants to make in the world. When core values are clearly defined and deeply ingrained in the company's DNA, they can serve as a powerful compass, guiding decision-making, inspiring employees, and attracting like-minded customers.

- **Clarity and Focus:** Core values provide clarity and focus, helping employees understand the company's priorities and make decisions that align with its mission.
- **Employee Engagement:** When employees feel connected to the

company's values, they are more likely to be engaged, motivated, and committed to their work.
- **Customer Loyalty:** Customers are increasingly drawn to brands that share their values. A strong set of core values can attract and retain customers who believe in the company's mission.
- **Reputation and Trust:** Companies with strong core values are often perceived as more trustworthy and reliable, enhancing their reputation and building long-term relationships with stakeholders.
- **Decision-Making:** In times of uncertainty or crisis, core values can serve as a guiding light, helping companies make difficult decisions that are consistent with their principles.

2. Identifying Your Core Values

Identifying your core values requires introspection, reflection, and open communication with your team. It is a process of discovering the fundamental beliefs and principles that are most important to you and your organisation. Here are some steps to guide you through the process:

- **Reflect on your personal values:** Start by identifying your own personal values. What are the principles that guide your life and decision-making?
- **Engage your team:** Involve your team in the process. Ask them to share their values and what they believe the company stands for.
- **Identify common themes:** Look for common themes and patterns in the values shared by you and your team. These commonalities can form the basis of your company's core values.
- **Craft concise statements:** Express your core values in clear and concise statements that are easy to understand and remember.
- **Live your values:** Make sure your core values are not just words on a wall. They should be integrated into your company's culture, decision-making, and actions.

3. The Power of Aspirations

While core values define what a company stands for in the present, aspirations represent its long-term vision and the positive impact it seeks to create in the world. Aspirations are ambitious goals that inspire and motivate, pushing the company to reach beyond its current capabilities and achieve something truly remarkable.

- **Inspiration and Motivation:** Aspirations inspire and motivate employees, giving them a sense of purpose and direction.
- **Innovation and Growth:** Ambitious goals can drive innovation and growth, pushing companies to explore new ideas and possibilities.
- **Attracting Talent:** A compelling vision can attract top talent who want to be part of something bigger than themselves.
- **Social Impact:** Aspirations that focus on creating a positive social or environmental impact can enhance the company's reputation and contribute to a better world.
- **Long-Term Success:** Aligning goals with a higher purpose can lead to long-term success, as companies that focus on creating value for all stakeholders are more likely to thrive in the long run.

4. Setting Aspirational Goals

Setting aspirational goals requires a combination of ambition, realism, and a deep understanding of your company's potential. Here are some tips for setting goals that inspire and motivate:

- **Think big:** Don't be afraid to dream big and set ambitious goals. The most successful companies are those that dare to imagine a better future.
- **Be specific:** Define your goals in clear and specific terms. This will help you track progress and measure success.
- **Make them measurable:** Set goals that can be measured and quantified. This will help you stay on track and make adjustments as needed.
- **Be realistic:** While it's important to be ambitious, your goals should also be realistic and achievable.
- **Align with your values:** Make sure your goals are aligned with your core values and aspirations. This will ensure that your pursuit of success is consistent with your purpose.

5. Aligning Your Goals with Excellence

Once you have defined your core values and aspirations, the next step is to align your goals with excellence. This means setting high standards for yourself and your team, and striving to achieve the best possible outcomes in everything you do.

- **Focus on quality:** Prioritise quality over quantity. Strive to deliver products or services that exceed customer expectations.
- **Continuous improvement:** Embrace a culture of continuous improvement. Always look for ways to improve your processes, products, and services.
- **Invest in your people:** Your employees are your most valuable asset. Invest in their development and empower them to reach their full potential.
- **Build strong relationships:** Cultivate strong relationships with your customers, suppliers, and other stakeholders. These relationships are essential for long-term success.
- **Give back to the community:** Support the communities in which you operate. This will enhance your reputation and create goodwill.

The power of purpose lies in its ability to align your goals with excellence. By discovering your core values and aspirations, and setting goals that are consistent with your purpose, you can create a business that is not only successful but also meaningful and impactful. Remember, true success is not just about achieving financial goals; it's about creating value for all stakeholders and making a positive contribution to the world.

Setting SMART Goals for Continuous Improvement

In the pursuit of excellence, businesses must embrace the philosophy of continuous improvement. This involves a relentless commitment to enhancing processes, products, and services, fostering a culture of innovation and growth. A powerful tool for achieving this is the setting of SMART goals - Specific, Measurable, Achievable, Relevant, and Time-bound. This section explores the concept of SMART goals in the context of continuous improvement, providing insights into how to formulate, implement, and track these goals to drive sustainable progress.

1. The Essence of SMART Goals

SMART goals provide a structured framework for setting and achieving objectives. They offer clarity, focus, and a sense of direction, enabling businesses to translate their aspirations into concrete actions. Each component of a SMART goal plays a vital role in its effectiveness:

- **Specific:** A SMART goal is clear and well-defined, leaving no room for ambiguity. It answers the questions of who, what, where, when, and why.
- **Measurable:** A SMART goal is quantifiable, allowing progress to be tracked and measured. This enables businesses to monitor their performance and make adjustments as needed.
- **Achievable:** A SMART goal is realistic and attainable, given the available resources and constraints. It challenges the business to stretch its capabilities without setting unattainable expectations.

- **Relevant:** A SMART goal is aligned with the overall business strategy and objectives. It contributes to the company's mission and vision.
- **Time-bound:** A SMART goal has a clear deadline or timeframe for completion. This creates a sense of urgency and helps maintain focus.

2. The Role of SMART Goals in Continuous Improvement

SMART goals are particularly valuable in the context of continuous improvement, as they provide a structured approach to identifying areas for enhancement, setting targets, and measuring progress. By setting SMART goals, businesses can:

- **Identify areas for improvement:** A thorough analysis of current processes, products, or services can reveal areas where improvements can be made. SMART goals can then be set to address these areas.
- **Set clear targets:** SMART goals provide clear and measurable targets, ensuring

everyone in the organisation understands what needs to be achieved.
- **Track progress:** The measurable nature of SMART goals allows businesses to track their progress and identify any roadblocks or challenges.
- **Celebrate successes:** Achieving SMART goals provides opportunities to celebrate successes and recognize the contributions of individuals and teams.
- **Foster a culture of continuous improvement:** The regular setting and achievement of SMART goals can create a culture where continuous improvement is valued and encouraged.

3. Formulating SMART Goals for Continuous Improvement

The process of formulating SMART goals for continuous improvement involves several key steps:

- **Identify the area for improvement:** Start by identifying the specific process, product, or service that you want to improve.

- **Gather data and insights:** Collect data and insights about the current state of the area you want to improve. This can involve analysing performance metrics, conducting surveys, or gathering feedback from customers and employees.
- **Set specific and measurable goals:** Based on your analysis, set specific and measurable goals that are aligned with your overall business objectives. Make sure your goals are achievable and relevant to your business.
- **Set a deadline:** Assign a clear deadline or timeframe for achieving your goals. This will create a sense of urgency and help maintain focus.
- **Communicate your goals:** Share your SMART goals with your team and ensure everyone understands their role in achieving them.
- **Track progress and make adjustments:** Regularly track your progress towards your goals and make adjustments as needed. Celebrate successes and learn from any setbacks.

4. Examples of SMART Goals for Continuous Improvement

Here are some examples of SMART goals that businesses can set for continuous improvement:

- **Increase customer satisfaction:**
    - Specific: Increase customer satisfaction scores by 10%.
    - Measurable: Track customer satisfaction scores through surveys and feedback.
    - Achievable: Implement customer service training programs and enhance communication channels.
    - Relevant: Improved customer satisfaction leads to increased loyalty and repeat business.
    - Time-bound: Achieve the 10% increase within six months.
- **Reduce production costs:**
    - Specific: Reduce production costs by 5% through process optimization.
    - Measurable: Track production costs and identify areas for improvement.
    - Achievable: Implement lean manufacturing principles and invest in new technologies.

- Relevant: Reduced production costs lead to increased profitability and competitiveness.
- Time-bound: Achieve the 5% reduction within one year.
- **Improve employee engagement:**
  - Specific: Increase employee engagement scores by 15% through various initiatives.
  - Measurable: Conduct employee surveys and gather feedback on engagement levels.
  - Achievable: Implement employee recognition programs, provide opportunities for growth and development, and foster a positive work environment.
  - Relevant: Increased employee engagement leads to higher productivity, innovation, and retention.
  - Time-bound: Achieve the 15% increase within nine months.

5. Overcoming Challenges in Setting and Achieving SMART Goals

While SMART goals offer a powerful framework for continuous improvement, there are also challenges that businesses may encounter:

- **Resistance to change:** Some employees may resist change or be hesitant to embrace new goals or processes.
- **Lack of resources:** Limited resources, such as time, budget, or personnel, can hinder the achievement of SMART goals.
- **Unforeseen circumstances:** Unexpected events or challenges can disrupt progress towards goals.
- **Lack of accountability:** If goals are not clearly communicated or ownership is not assigned, it can lead to a lack of accountability and hinder progress.

To overcome these challenges, businesses can:

- **Foster a culture of open communication:** Encourage open communication and feedback, addressing any concerns or resistance to change.
- **Provide adequate resources:** Ensure that sufficient resources are allocated to

support the achievement of SMART goals.
- **Be flexible and adaptable:** Be prepared to adjust goals or strategies in response to unforeseen circumstances.
- **Establish clear accountability:** Assign ownership of goals and ensure everyone understands their role in achieving them.
- **Celebrate successes and learn from setbacks:** Recognize and celebrate achievements, and use setbacks as opportunities for learning and growth.

Setting SMART goals is a powerful tool for driving continuous improvement in any business. By formulating clear, measurable, achievable, relevant, and time-bound goals, businesses can create a roadmap for progress, track their performance, and foster a culture of innovation and growth. While challenges may arise, overcoming them through open communication, resource allocation, flexibility, accountability, and a focus on learning can lead to sustainable success and a commitment to excellence.

Chapter 5

Embracing a Growth Mindset: Fostering a Love for Learning

Overcoming the Fixed Mindset: Challenges and Opportunities

In the ever-evolving landscape of business, a growth mindset is not just an advantage; it is a necessity. This chapter delves into the power of embracing a growth mindset, exploring its impact on individual and organisational development, and highlighting the challenges and opportunities associated with overcoming the fixed mindset.

Overcoming the Fixed Mindset: Challenges and Opportunities

A fixed mindset is the belief that abilities and intelligence are static and unchangeable. It fosters a fear of failure, a reluctance to take risks, and a tendency to avoid challenges. On the other hand, a growth mindset views abilities and intelligence as malleable and capable of development through dedication and hard work. It encourages a love for learning, a willingness to embrace challenges, and a resilience in the face of setbacks.

Challenges of the Fixed Mindset:

- **Fear of Failure:** Individuals with a fixed mindset often fear failure, as they see it as a reflection of their inherent abilities. This fear can lead to avoidance of challenges and missed opportunities for growth.
- **Limiting Beliefs:** Fixed mindset individuals may hold limiting beliefs about their potential, hindering their willingness to step outside their comfort zone and explore new possibilities.
- **Lack of Effort:** When faced with challenges, those with a fixed mindset may give up easily, believing that their efforts are futile.
- **Comparison and Competition:** Fixed mindset individuals may focus on comparing themselves to others, leading to feelings of inadequacy and a reluctance to collaborate.

- **Resistance to Feedback:** Feedback can be perceived as a threat to self-worth, leading to defensiveness and a missed opportunity for learning and improvement.

Opportunities of the Growth Mindset:

- **Embracing Challenges:** A growth mindset encourages individuals to embrace challenges as opportunities for learning and growth.
- **Resilience in the Face of Setbacks:** Setbacks are viewed as learning experiences, fostering resilience and a determination to persevere.
- **Focus on Effort and Learning:** The growth mindset emphasises the importance of effort and continuous learning, leading to a greater sense of control and empowerment.
- **Collaboration and Support:** Growth mindset individuals are more likely to seek collaboration and support, recognizing the value of diverse perspectives and shared learning.
- **Openness to Feedback:** Feedback is seen as a valuable tool for improvement,

leading to a greater willingness to learn and adapt.

Overcoming the Fixed Mindset:

Transitioning from a fixed to a growth mindset is a journey that requires effort and intentionality. Here are some strategies to foster a growth mindset:

- **Cultivate a Love for Learning:** Embrace curiosity, seek out new knowledge and skills, and view learning as a lifelong pursuit.
- **Embrace Challenges:** Step outside your comfort zone and take on challenges that stretch your abilities.
- **Celebrate Effort and Progress:** Focus on the effort you put in and the progress you make, rather than solely on the end result.
- **Reframe Failure as a Learning Opportunity:** View setbacks as opportunities to learn and grow, rather than as reflections of your inherent abilities.
- **Seek Feedback:** Actively seek feedback from others and use it constructively to improve your performance.

- **Surround Yourself with Growth-Minded Individuals:** Seek out mentors, colleagues, and friends who embody a growth mindset and can inspire and support your journey.
- **Practice Self-Compassion:** Be kind to yourself when you encounter challenges or setbacks. Remember that everyone makes mistakes and that learning is a process.

Impact of a Growth Mindset:

Embracing a growth mindset can have a profound impact on both individuals and organisations:

- **Individual Growth and Development:** A growth mindset fuels personal and professional development, enabling individuals to reach their full potential.
- **Increased Motivation and Engagement:** The belief in the possibility of growth fosters intrinsic motivation and a greater sense of purpose.
- **Enhanced Creativity and Innovation:** A growth mindset encourages

experimentation and risk-taking, leading to greater creativity and innovation.
- **Improved Collaboration and Teamwork:** The willingness to learn from others and embrace diverse perspectives fosters collaboration and teamwork.
- **Organisational Success:** A growth mindset culture can lead to increased productivity, innovation, and adaptability, driving organisational success.

In today's rapidly changing world, a growth mindset is essential for individuals and organisations to thrive. By overcoming the limitations of the fixed mindset and embracing a love for learning, individuals can unlock their full potential, achieve their goals, and contribute to a more innovative and successful future.

Developing Effective Learning Strategies

In the pursuit of knowledge and skills, the journey of learning is a lifelong endeavour. However, the effectiveness of this journey hinges upon the strategies employed. This chapter delves into the realm of effective learning strategies, exploring a diverse range of techniques and approaches that can empower individuals to optimise their learning experiences, enhance their retention, and achieve their educational goals.

1. The Foundations of Effective Learning

Before diving into specific learning strategies, it is crucial to understand the foundational principles that underpin effective learning. These principles provide a framework for maximising the learning process and ensuring that knowledge is acquired, retained, and applied effectively.

- **Active Engagement:** Effective learning is an active process that requires engagement and participation. It involves more than just passively absorbing information; it entails actively interacting with the material, asking questions, and seeking connections.
- **Metacognition:** Metacognition refers to the awareness and understanding of one's own thought processes. It involves monitoring one's learning, identifying

strengths and weaknesses, and adjusting strategies accordingly.
- **Motivation and Goal Setting:** Motivation plays a vital role in driving the learning process. Setting clear and achievable goals can provide direction and purpose, fueling the desire to learn and achieve.
- **Feedback and Reflection:** Feedback provides valuable insights into one's learning progress, highlighting areas for improvement and reinforcing strengths. Reflection allows for deeper understanding and internalisation of knowledge.
- **Practice and Application:** Learning is not just about acquiring knowledge; it's about applying it in real-world contexts. Practice and application solidify understanding and facilitate the transfer of knowledge to new situations.

2. A Diverse Toolkit of Learning Strategies

There is no one-size-fits-all approach to learning. Different individuals have different learning styles, preferences, and strengths. Therefore, it is essential to have a diverse toolkit of learning strategies at your disposal, enabling you to adapt your approach to different situations and subjects.

2.1 Active Learning Strategies

Active learning strategies involve actively engaging with the material, rather than passively receiving information. These strategies can enhance understanding, retention, and application of knowledge.

- **Note-Taking:** Taking notes during lectures, readings, or discussions can help you organise information, identify key points, and facilitate review later.
- **Summarization:** Summarising information in your own words can help you synthesise key concepts and test your understanding.
- **Questioning:** Asking questions about the material can help you clarify concepts, deepen your understanding, and stimulate critical thinking.
- **Discussion and Collaboration:** Engaging in discussions and collaborating with peers can provide opportunities for active

learning, sharing ideas, and gaining new perspectives.
- **Problem-Solving and Application:** Applying knowledge to solve problems or complete tasks can help solidify understanding and demonstrate practical application.

2.2 Metacognitive Strategies

Metacognitive strategies involve monitoring and regulating your own learning processes. These strategies can help you identify your strengths and weaknesses, adjust your approach, and optimise your learning experience.

- **Planning:** Before starting a learning task, take some time to plan your approach. Consider the goals, the resources available, and the strategies you will use.
- **Monitoring:** While learning, pay attention to your understanding and identify any areas where you are struggling.
- **Evaluating:** After completing a learning task, evaluate your performance and identify areas for improvement.

- **Adjusting:** Based on your evaluation, adjust your strategies and approach for future learning tasks.

2.3 Motivation and Goal-Setting Strategies

Motivation is a key driver of learning. Setting clear and achievable goals can provide direction and purpose, fueling the desire to learn and achieve.

- **Set SMART Goals:** Set Specific, Measurable, Achievable, Relevant, and Time-bound goals. This will help you stay focused and motivated.
- **Break Down Large Goals into Smaller Steps:** This can make goals seem less daunting and more manageable.
- **Celebrate Progress:** Recognize and celebrate your achievements along the way. This can help maintain motivation and build confidence.
- **Find Your Intrinsic Motivation:** Identify what personally motivates you to learn and tap into that intrinsic drive.
- **Seek Support and Encouragement:** Surround yourself with supportive

individuals who can encourage and motivate you.

2.4 Feedback and Reflection Strategies

Feedback and reflection are essential for learning and growth. They provide opportunities to assess your understanding, identify areas for improvement, and solidify your knowledge.

- **Seek Feedback:** Actively seek feedback from teachers, peers, or mentors.
- **Reflect on Your Learning:** Take time to reflect on what you have learned, how you learned it, and what you can improve.
- **Use Feedback to Adjust Your Approach:** Use feedback to identify areas where you need to improve and adjust your learning strategies accordingly.
- **Keep a Learning Journal:** Document your learning journey, including your goals, challenges, successes, and reflections.

2.5 Practice and Application Strategies

Practice and application are crucial for solidifying understanding and facilitating the transfer of knowledge to new situations.

- **Practice Regularly:** Consistent practice is key to mastering new skills and knowledge.
- **Apply Knowledge to Real-World Contexts:** Seek opportunities to apply what you have learned to real-world situations.
- **Teach Others:** Teaching others can help you deepen your own understanding and identify any gaps in your knowledge.
- **Seek Opportunities for Hands-On Learning:** Engage in activities that allow you to practise and apply your knowledge in a hands-on way.

3. Adapting Learning Strategies to Different Contexts

The effectiveness of learning strategies can vary depending on the context, including the subject matter, the learning environment, and the individual's learning style. It is important to be flexible and adaptable in your approach, tailoring your strategies to suit the specific situation.

- **Subject Matter:** Different subjects may require different learning strategies. For

example, memorization may be more effective for learning vocabulary, while problem-solving may be more effective for learning maths.
- **Learning Environment:** The learning environment can also influence the effectiveness of different strategies. For example, group work may be more effective in a collaborative classroom setting, while independent study may be more effective in a quiet library.
- **Learning Style:** Individuals have different learning styles, such as visual, auditory, or kinesthetic. It is important to identify your own learning style and choose strategies that are compatible with your preferences.

4. Technology and Learning

Technology has revolutionised the way we learn, providing access to a wealth of information and resources. However, it is important to use technology strategically and mindfully to enhance, rather than hinder, the learning process.

- **Online Courses and Resources:** Online courses and resources can provide flexible and accessible learning opportunities.
- **Learning Apps and Tools:** There are numerous apps and tools available to support learning, such as flashcard apps, note-taking apps, and language learning apps.
- **Social Media and Online Communities:** Social media and online communities can provide opportunities for collaboration, discussion, and knowledge sharing.
- **Mindful Technology Use:** It is important to be mindful of how you use technology and avoid distractions. Set boundaries and create a conducive learning environment.

The journey of learning is a lifelong pursuit that requires dedication, effort, and effective strategies. By understanding the foundations of effective learning, embracing a diverse toolkit of strategies, adapting your approach to different contexts, and utilising technology mindfully, you can optimise your learning experience, enhance your retention, and achieve your educational goals. Remember, learning is not just about acquiring knowledge; it's about growing, evolving, and reaching your full potential.

CHAPTER 6

Building Resilience: Overcoming Obstacles on the Path to Excellence

Embracing Failure as a Stepping Stone

In the relentless pursuit of excellence, the journey is rarely smooth. Challenges, setbacks, and failures are inevitable companions along the way. However, it is in the face of these obstacles that true resilience is forged. This chapter explores the concept of resilience in the context of achieving excellence, emphasising the importance of embracing failure as a stepping stone to growth and success.

Embracing Failure as a Stepping Stone

Failure, often perceived as a negative and discouraging experience, can be reframed as a valuable learning opportunity. It is through setbacks and mistakes that we gain insights, develop new strategies, and ultimately achieve greater heights. Embracing failure as a stepping stone involves a shift in perspective, viewing it not as an endpoint but as a catalyst for growth.

1. The Fear of Failure

The fear of failure is a common obstacle that can hinder progress and prevent individuals from reaching their full potential. It can manifest in various ways, such as:

- **Procrastination:** Putting off tasks or projects due to fear of not being able to complete them perfectly.
- **Perfectionism:** Striving for unattainable standards, leading to anxiety and frustration.
- **Risk Aversion:** Avoiding challenges or opportunities that carry the potential for failure.
- **Self-Doubt:** Questioning one's abilities and fearing judgement from others.

These manifestations of the fear of failure can create a self-fulfilling prophecy, limiting opportunities for growth and hindering progress towards excellence.

2. Reframing Failure

To overcome the fear of failure and embrace it as a stepping stone, a shift in perspective is necessary. Here are some key reframing strategies:

- **Failure as Feedback:** View failure not as a personal shortcoming but as valuable feedback that provides insights into areas for improvement.
- **Failure as a Learning Opportunity:** See failure as a chance to learn, grow, and develop new strategies.
- **Failure as a Part of the Process:** Recognize that failure is a natural part of the journey towards excellence. Even the most successful individuals and organisations have experienced setbacks along the way.
- **Failure as a Catalyst for Growth:** Embrace failure as a catalyst for personal and professional growth. It can lead to greater resilience, adaptability, and innovation.

3. Cultivating Resilience

Resilience is the ability to bounce back from adversity, learn from setbacks, and continue moving forward towards your goals. It is a key ingredient for achieving excellence in any endeavour. Here are some strategies for cultivating resilience:

- **Develop a Growth Mindset:** Embrace the belief that abilities and intelligence can be developed through dedication and hard work.
- **Set Realistic Expectations:** Set achievable goals and recognize that progress takes time and effort.
- **Build a Support Network:** Surround yourself with supportive individuals who can offer encouragement and guidance during challenging times.
- **Practice Self-Care:** Prioritise your physical and mental well-being through healthy habits and stress management techniques.
- **Learn from Your Mistakes:** Reflect on your setbacks, identify lessons learned, and apply those insights to future endeavours.
- **Celebrate Small Wins:** Acknowledge and celebrate your progress, no matter how small.

- **Maintain a Positive Attitude:** Cultivate optimism and focus on the possibilities, even in the face of adversity.

4. The Power of Perseverance

Perseverance is the steadfast pursuit of a goal despite challenges, obstacles, or discouragement. It is the unwavering determination to continue moving forward, even when the path seems difficult or uncertain. Perseverance is a key component of resilience and a crucial ingredient for achieving excellence.

- **Setbacks as Motivation:** View setbacks as opportunities to re-evaluate your strategies, learn from your mistakes, and come back stronger.
- **Focus on the Long-Term:** Keep your long-term goals in mind and don't let short-term setbacks derail your progress.
- **Find Inspiration:** Seek inspiration from others who have overcome challenges and achieved success.
- **Break Down Goals into Smaller Steps:** Make your goals more manageable by breaking them down into smaller, achievable steps.

- **Celebrate Progress:** Acknowledge and celebrate your progress along the way, no matter how small.

5. Examples of Resilience in Action

Throughout history, there are countless examples of individuals and organisations that have demonstrated remarkable resilience in the face of adversity.

- **J.K. Rowling:** The author of the Harry Potter series faced numerous rejections before finding a publisher. Her perseverance and belief in her work ultimately led to global success.
- **Steve Jobs:** After being ousted from Apple, the company he co-founded, Steve Jobs went on to create Pixar and NeXT, eventually returning to Apple and leading it to unprecedented success.
- **Malala Yousafzai:** The youngest Nobel Prize laureate, Malala Yousafzai, survived a Taliban assassination attempt and continues to advocate for education for girls around the world.
- **The Wright Brothers:** The inventors of the aeroplane faced countless setbacks and

failures before achieving their dream of powered flight.

These examples illustrate the power of resilience in overcoming obstacles and achieving remarkable feats.

In the pursuit of excellence, resilience is not just an asset; it is a necessity. By embracing failure as a stepping stone, cultivating resilience, and persevering in the face of challenges, individuals and organisations can overcome obstacles, learn from their mistakes, and ultimately achieve their goals. Remember, the journey to excellence is not a straight line; it is a winding path filled with twists and turns. But with resilience and determination, you can navigate any challenge and emerge stronger and more successful than ever before.

Developing Strategies for Overcoming Challenges

In the pursuit of any goal, challenges are inevitable. They can arise from various sources, including internal factors, external circumstances, or unexpected events. This chapter delves into the strategies and approaches individuals and organisations can employ to overcome challenges effectively, fostering resilience, adaptability, and a relentless drive towards success.

1. The Nature of Challenges

Challenges come in various forms and can manifest at different stages of the journey toward a goal. Understanding the nature of challenges is crucial for developing effective strategies to overcome them.

1.1 Internal Challenges

Internal challenges originate from within an individual or organisation. They can include:

- **Lack of skills or knowledge:** The absence of necessary skills or knowledge can hinder progress and create obstacles.
- **Fear and self-doubt:** Negative emotions, such as fear of failure or self-doubt, can paralyse action and prevent individuals from taking risks.

- **Procrastination and lack of motivation:** Procrastination and a lack of motivation can lead to delays and missed opportunities.
- **Limited resources:** Insufficient resources, such as time, money, or personnel, can pose challenges to achieving goals.
- **Internal conflicts:** Disagreements or conflicts within a team or organisation can create roadblocks and impede progress.

1.2 External Challenges

External challenges stem from factors outside the control of an individual or organisation. These can include:

- **Economic downturns:** Economic recessions or downturns can impact businesses, leading to reduced demand, financial constraints, and job losses.
- **Market competition:** Intense competition can pose challenges for businesses, requiring them to constantly innovate and differentiate themselves.
- **Technological disruptions:** Rapid technological advancements can disrupt

industries and render existing skills or products obsolete.
- **Natural disasters or unforeseen events:** Natural disasters, pandemics, or other unforeseen events can create disruptions and challenges for individuals and organisations.
- **Regulatory changes:** Changes in laws or regulations can impact businesses, requiring them to adapt their operations or strategies.

2. Strategies for Overcoming Challenges

While challenges are inevitable, they are not insurmountable. By developing and implementing effective strategies, individuals and organisations can overcome obstacles and achieve their goals.

2.1 Proactive Strategies

Proactive strategies involve anticipating and preparing for potential challenges before they arise. These strategies can help mitigate risks and enhance resilience.

- **Risk assessment and mitigation:** Identify potential risks and develop plans to address them before they occur.
- **Contingency planning:** Create backup plans or alternative strategies in case the original plan encounters obstacles.
- **Building a strong foundation:** Invest in developing skills, knowledge, and resources that can help navigate challenges.
- **Cultivating a positive mindset:** Foster a positive and optimistic outlook, focusing on solutions rather than dwelling on problems.
- **Building a support network:** Surround yourself with supportive individuals who can offer guidance and encouragement during challenging times.

2.2 Reactive Strategies

Reactive strategies are employed when challenges arise unexpectedly. These strategies focus on adapting and responding effectively to the situation at hand.

- **Problem-solving and critical thinking:** Analyse the challenge, identify its root causes, and develop creative solutions.
- **Flexibility and adaptability:** Be willing to adjust plans and strategies as needed to respond to changing circumstances.
- **Seeking help and support:** Don't hesitate to seek help from others, whether it's from colleagues, mentors, or external experts.
- **Learning from setbacks:** View setbacks as opportunities for learning and growth, and apply those lessons to future endeavours.
- **Maintaining a positive attitude:** Even in the face of adversity, maintain a positive attitude and focus on finding solutions.

2.3 Specific Strategies for Overcoming Common Challenges

- **Lack of skills or knowledge:** Invest in training and development programs to acquire the necessary skills or knowledge.
- **Fear and self-doubt:** Challenge negative thoughts and beliefs, practice self-compassion, and seek support from mentors or coaches.

- **Procrastination and lack of motivation:** Break down tasks into smaller, more manageable steps, set deadlines, and reward yourself for progress.
- **Limited resources:** Prioritise and allocate resources strategically, seek external funding or partnerships, and leverage technology to improve efficiency.
- **Internal conflicts:** Foster open communication, encourage collaboration, and seek mediation or conflict resolution if needed.
- **Economic downturns:** Diversify your business, reduce costs, and focus on providing value to customers.
- **Market competition:** Innovate, differentiate your offerings, and build strong customer relationships.
- **Technological disruptions:** Stay informed about emerging technologies, invest in training and development, and adapt your business model as needed.
- **Natural disasters or unforeseen events:** Have a crisis management plan in place, communicate effectively with stakeholders, and focus on recovery and rebuilding.

- **Regulatory changes:** Stay informed about regulatory changes, seek legal advice if needed, and adapt your operations or strategies to comply with new requirements.

3. The Role of Mindset

A positive and resilient mindset is crucial for overcoming challenges. It involves:

- **Embracing a growth mindset:** Believing that abilities and intelligence can be developed through dedication and hard work.
- **Focusing on solutions:** Shifting your focus from problems to solutions and opportunities.
- **Maintaining optimism:** Cultivating a positive outlook and believing in your ability to overcome challenges.
- **Learning from setbacks:** Viewing setbacks as opportunities for growth and learning.
- **Celebrating successes:** Acknowledging and celebrating your achievements, no matter how small.

4. Case Studies of Overcoming Challenges

Numerous individuals and organisations have demonstrated remarkable resilience in overcoming challenges and achieving success. Their stories can serve as inspiration and provide valuable lessons.

- **Oprah Winfrey:** Overcoming a difficult childhood and numerous setbacks, Oprah Winfrey built a media empire and became one of the most influential people in the world.
- **Apple:** After facing near bankruptcy in the late 1990s, Apple rebounded under the leadership of Steve Jobs, becoming one of the most valuable companies in the world.
- **Malala Yousafzai:** Despite being shot by the Taliban for advocating for education for girls, Malala Yousafzai continued her fight and became a global symbol of courage and resilience.
- **The COVID-19 pandemic:** The pandemic posed unprecedented challenges for businesses and individuals around the world. However, many demonstrated remarkable adaptability and resilience, finding new ways to operate and thrive.

Challenges are an inevitable part of life and business. However, they do not have to be insurmountable. By developing and implementing effective strategies, cultivating a resilient mindset, and learning from setbacks, individuals and organisations can overcome obstacles and achieve their goals. Remember, challenges are not roadblocks; they are opportunities for growth, learning, and innovation. Embrace them, learn from them, and emerge stronger and more successful than ever before.

Part III

Mastering the Art of Excellence In Action

Chapter 7

Crafting a Personalized Action Plan: Putting Theory into Practice

Identifying Key Areas for Improvement

In the preceding chapters, we explored a plethora of concepts, strategies, and insights aimed at fostering a culture of excellence and continuous improvement. However, the true power of these ideas lies in their practical application. This chapter focuses on translating theory into action by crafting a personalised action plan, beginning with the crucial step of identifying key areas for improvement.

Identifying Key Areas for Improvement

The first step in creating an effective action plan is to identify the specific areas where improvement is needed. This involves a thorough and honest assessment of your current situation, strengths, weaknesses, and opportunities for growth. By pinpointing the areas that require attention, you can focus your efforts and resources on making meaningful progress towards your goals.

1. Conducting a Self-Assessment

A self-assessment is a critical tool for gaining a deeper understanding of your current state and identifying areas for improvement. It involves reflecting on your performance, skills, knowledge, and habits, and evaluating them against your goals and aspirations. Here are some key questions to guide your self-assessment:

- **What are my strengths and weaknesses?** Identify the areas where you excel and those where you need to improve.
- **What are my current skills and knowledge?** Assess your current skills and knowledge base, and identify any gaps that need to be filled.
- **What are my goals and aspirations?** Clarify your short-term and long-term goals, both personally and professionally.

- **What are my habits and behaviours?** Reflect on your daily habits and behaviours, and identify any patterns that may be hindering your progress.
- **What feedback have I received from others?** Consider feedback from colleagues, mentors, or supervisors, and identify any recurring themes or areas for improvement.

2. Analysing Performance Data

In addition to self-assessment, analysing performance data can provide valuable insights into areas for improvement. This data can include:

- **Key Performance Indicators (KPIs):** Track and analyse your performance on key metrics relevant to your goals.
- **Customer feedback:** Gather and analyse feedback from customers to identify areas where you can improve your products or services.
- **Employee feedback:** Seek feedback from your employees to identify areas where you can improve your leadership, communication, or organisational culture.

- **Industry benchmarks:** Compare your performance to industry benchmarks to identify areas where you may be lagging behind.

3. Identifying Root Causes

Once you have identified areas for improvement, it is essential to delve deeper and identify the root causes of these issues. This will help you develop targeted solutions and prevent the same problems from recurring in the future. Consider the following questions:

- **Why is this an area for improvement?** What are the underlying factors contributing to the issue?
- **What are the consequences of not addressing this issue?** How will it impact your performance, goals, or overall success?
- **What are the potential benefits of addressing this issue?** How will it contribute to your growth and development?

4. Prioritising Areas for Improvement

After identifying several areas for improvement, it is important to prioritise them based on their impact and urgency. This will help you focus your efforts and resources on the most critical areas first. Consider the following factors when prioritising:

- **Impact:** How significantly will addressing this issue impact your overall goals and success?
- **Urgency:** How quickly does this issue need to be addressed?
- **Feasibility:** How feasible is it to address this issue given your current resources and constraints?
- **Alignment with values:** How well does addressing this issue align with your core values and aspirations?

5. Setting SMART Goals

Once you have identified and prioritised your key areas for improvement, it's time to set SMART goals to guide your actions. As discussed in the previous chapter, SMART goals are:

- **Specific:** Clearly define what you want to achieve.

- **Measurable:** Establish criteria for measuring progress and success.
- **Achievable:** Set realistic and attainable goals given your resources and constraints.
- **Relevant:** Ensure your goals align with your overall objectives and contribute to your long-term vision.
- **Time-bound:** Set a deadline or timeframe for achieving your goals.

By setting SMART goals, you create a roadmap for improvement, providing clarity, focus, and a sense of direction.

Identifying key areas for improvement is a crucial step in crafting a personalised action plan for achieving excellence. By conducting a self-assessment, analysing performance data, identifying root causes, prioritising areas for improvement, and setting SMART goals, you can create a targeted and effective plan that will guide you towards your desired outcomes. Remember, the journey to excellence is a continuous process of learning, growth, and adaptation. By embracing challenges, seeking feedback, and remaining committed to your goals, you can overcome obstacles and achieve remarkable success.

Developing Actionable Steps and Milestones

Once you have identified and prioritised your key areas for improvement, it is essential to translate your goals into actionable steps and milestones. This chapter focuses on creating a clear and structured action plan, breaking down your goals into manageable tasks, and establishing milestones to track your progress along the way.

1. The Importance of Actionable Steps

Setting goals is important, but without actionable steps, they remain mere aspirations. Actionable steps provide a roadmap for achieving your goals, breaking them down into smaller, more manageable tasks that can be tackled systematically. By defining clear and specific actions, you create a sense of direction, focus, and accountability.

Benefits of Actionable Steps:

- **Clarity and Focus:** Actionable steps provide clarity on what needs to be done, eliminating ambiguity and confusion.
- **Motivation and Momentum:** Breaking down goals into smaller tasks creates a sense of progress and momentum, boosting motivation.
- **Accountability and Responsibility:** Assigning ownership of specific tasks fosters accountability and responsibility.
- **Flexibility and Adaptability:** Actionable steps allow for flexibility and adaptation in response to changing circumstances or unexpected challenges.
- **Measurable Progress:** By tracking the completion of actionable steps, you can measure progress towards your goals.

2. Creating an Action Plan

An action plan is a structured document that outlines the specific steps, tasks, and resources required to achieve a goal. It serves as a roadmap, guiding your efforts and ensuring that you stay on track. Here are some key elements of an effective action plan:

- **Goal Statement:** Clearly articulate the goal you want to achieve.
- **Action Steps:** Break down the goal into smaller, actionable steps.
- **Timeline:** Assign deadlines or timeframes for each step.
- **Resources:** Identify the resources required for each step, such as personnel, budget, or technology.
- **Metrics:** Define the metrics or KPIs that will be used to measure progress and success.
- **Contingency Plans:** Anticipate potential challenges or obstacles and develop contingency plans to address them.

3. Setting Milestones

Milestones are significant points or achievements along the path to your goal. They serve as markers of progress, providing opportunities to celebrate successes, evaluate your strategies, and make adjustments as needed.

Benefits of Milestones:

- **Motivation and Encouragement:** Reaching milestones provides a sense of accomplishment and boosts motivation.

- **Progress Tracking:** Milestones allow you to track your progress towards your goal and identify any areas where you may be falling behind.
- **Evaluation and Adjustment:** Milestones offer opportunities to evaluate your strategies and make adjustments as needed to ensure you stay on track.
- **Communication and Collaboration:** Milestones provide a framework for communicating progress to stakeholders and fostering collaboration within teams.

4. Key Considerations for Developing Actionable Steps and Milestones

When developing actionable steps and milestones, it is essential to consider the following factors:

- **Specificity:** Each step and milestone should be specific and clearly defined, leaving no room for ambiguity.
- **Measurability:** Establish clear criteria for measuring progress and success for each step and milestone.

- **Achievability:** Ensure that each step and milestone is realistic and attainable, given your resources and constraints.
- **Relevance:** Align each step and milestone with your overall goal and ensure they contribute to your long-term vision.
- **Time-bound:** Assign deadlines or timeframes for each step and milestone, creating a sense of urgency and focus.
- **Flexibility:** Be prepared to adjust your action plan and milestones as needed in response to changing circumstances or unexpected challenges.
- **Collaboration:** Involve relevant stakeholders in the development and implementation of your action plan, fostering a sense of ownership and shared responsibility.
- **Communication:** Regularly communicate progress and updates on milestones to ensure everyone is aligned and informed.
- **Celebration:** Recognize and celebrate the achievement of milestones to boost morale and maintain motivation.

5. Examples of Actionable Steps and Milestones

Here are some examples of how to break down goals into actionable steps and milestones:

- **Goal: Launch a new product within six months.**
  - Action Steps:
    - Conduct market research and identify target audience.
    - Develop product concept and design.
    - Create a marketing and launch plan.
    - Secure necessary funding and resources.
    - Manufacture and distribute the product.
  - Milestones:
    - Completion of market research and target audience identification.
    - Finalisation of product concept and design.
    - Approval of marketing and launch plan.
    - Securing funding and resources.
    - Successful product launch.

- **Goal: Increase customer satisfaction by 15% within one year.**
    - Action Steps:
        - Conduct customer surveys to gather feedback.
        - Analyse feedback and identify areas for improvement.
        - Implement customer service training programs.
        - Enhance communication channels with customers.
        - Monitor and track customer satisfaction scores.
    - Milestones:
        - Completion of customer surveys and feedback analysis.
        - Implementation of customer service training programs.
        - Enhancement of communication channels.
        - Achievement of a 5% increase in customer satisfaction within six months.

- Achievement of a 15% increase in customer satisfaction within one year.
- **Goal: Reduce employee turnover by 10% within two years.**
  - Action Steps:
    - Conduct exit interviews to understand reasons for turnover.
    - Analyse feedback and identify areas for improvement.
    - Implement employee engagement and recognition programs.
    - Provide opportunities for growth and development.
    - Foster a positive and inclusive work environment.
  - Milestones:
    - Completion of exit interviews and feedback analysis.
    - Implementation of employee engagement and recognition programs.
    - Creation of opportunities for growth and development.

- Achievement of a 5% reduction in employee turnover within one year.
- Achievement of a 10% reduction in employee turnover within two years.

Developing actionable steps and milestones is a crucial step in translating your goals into reality. By breaking down your goals into manageable tasks, setting clear milestones, and tracking your progress along the way, you can create a roadmap for success and ensure that you stay on track towards achieving excellence. Remember, the journey to excellence is a marathon, not a sprint. By taking consistent action, celebrating milestones, and adapting to challenges, you can achieve remarkable results and realise your full potential.

Chapter 8

Cultivating Effective Habits: The Building Blocks of Excellence

Identifying Essential Habits for Your Chosen Field

Excellence is not a destination but a journey, paved with consistent effort, dedication, and the cultivation of effective habits. This chapter explores the profound impact of habits on personal and professional growth, emphasising the importance of identifying and adopting essential habits that can propel individuals towards excellence in their chosen field.

Identifying Essential Habits for Your Chosen Field

While the specific habits required for excellence may vary across different fields, there are certain fundamental habits that are universally applicable and can significantly contribute to success. This section focuses on identifying these essential habits and understanding their significance in fostering a culture of excellence.

1. The Power of Habits

Habits are deeply ingrained patterns of behaviour that are performed automatically and unconsciously. They shape our thoughts, actions, and ultimately, our outcomes. By cultivating effective habits, we can create a foundation for success, enabling us to perform at our best consistently.

- **Efficiency and Productivity:** Effective habits streamline our actions, allowing us to accomplish more in less time and with less effort.
- **Focus and Concentration:** Habits help us develop focus and concentration, enabling us to minimise distractions and stay on task.
- **Discipline and Self-Control:** Habits foster discipline and self-control, enabling us to resist temptations and stay committed to our goals.
- **Continuous Improvement:** Habits create a framework for continuous improvement,

enabling us to refine our skills and knowledge over time.
- **Positive Mindset:** Effective habits can contribute to a positive mindset, promoting optimism, resilience, and a belief in one's abilities.

2. Identifying Essential Habits

The specific habits required for excellence will vary depending on your chosen field. However, some fundamental habits are universally applicable and can contribute significantly to success in any endeavour.

- **Goal Setting and Planning:** Setting clear and achievable goals, and developing a plan to reach them, is crucial for success.
- **Time Management:** Effective time management allows you to prioritise tasks, avoid procrastination, and make the most of your time.
- **Continuous Learning:** A commitment to lifelong learning enables you to stay ahead of the curve, adapt to change, and expand your knowledge and skills.
- **Effective Communication:** Strong communication skills are essential for

building relationships, collaborating with others, and conveying your ideas clearly.
- **Problem-Solving and Critical Thinking:** The ability to analyse situations, identify problems, and develop effective solutions is crucial for success in any field.
- **Adaptability and Resilience:** The ability to adapt to change, overcome challenges, and bounce back from setbacks is essential for navigating the complexities of the modern world.
- **Self-Discipline and Motivation:** Self-discipline and motivation are key drivers of success, enabling you to stay focused, overcome obstacles, and achieve your goals.
- **Networking and Collaboration:** Building relationships and collaborating with others can open doors to new opportunities and provide valuable support and insights.
- **Health and Wellness:** Prioritising your physical and mental health is essential for maintaining energy, focus, and overall well-being.

3. Identifying Habits Specific to Your Field

In addition to the fundamental habits mentioned above, it is essential to identify the specific habits that are most relevant to your chosen field. This requires a deep understanding of the skills, knowledge, and behaviours that are valued and rewarded in your industry.

- **Research and Observation:** Conduct research, observe successful individuals in your field, and seek guidance from mentors or experts to identify the habits that contribute to their success.
- **Self-Reflection:** Reflect on your own experiences and identify the habits that have helped you achieve your goals in the past.
- **Seek Feedback:** Ask colleagues, supervisors, or mentors for feedback on your strengths and weaknesses, and identify areas where you can develop new habits.
- **Experiment and Adapt:** Be willing to experiment with different habits and adapt your approach based on your experiences and feedback.

4. Developing and Implementing Habits

Once you have identified the essential habits for your chosen field, it is time to develop and implement them into your daily routine. This requires commitment, discipline, and a willingness to embrace change.

- **Start Small:** Begin by focusing on one or two habits at a time. Trying to change too many things at once can be overwhelming and lead to frustration.
- **Create a Plan:** Develop a clear plan for how you will implement your new habits. Set specific goals, identify triggers, and establish rewards for success.
- **Track Your Progress:** Monitor your progress and make adjustments as needed. Celebrate your successes and learn from your setbacks.
- **Be Patient and Persistent:** Developing new habits takes time and effort. Be patient with yourself and don't give up if you experience setbacks.
- **Seek Support:** Surround yourself with supportive individuals who can encourage and motivate you along the way.

5. Overcoming Challenges

Developing new habits can be challenging, and setbacks are inevitable. However, by anticipating and addressing these challenges proactively, you can increase your chances of success.

- **Lack of Motivation:** Find ways to stay motivated, such as setting reminders, visualising your goals, or rewarding yourself for progress.
- **Time Constraints:** Make time for your new habits by prioritising them and eliminating non-essential activities.
- **Environmental Factors:** Create an environment that supports your new habits, minimising distractions and temptations.
- **Setbacks and Relapses:** Don't be discouraged by setbacks or relapses. View them as learning opportunities and recommit to your goals.

Cultivating effective habits is a powerful tool for achieving excellence in any field. By identifying essential habits, developing and implementing them into your daily routine, and overcoming challenges along the way, you can create a foundation for success, unlock your full potential, and achieve your goals. Remember, habits are not built overnight; they require consistent effort, dedication, and a willingness to embrace change. But with perseverance and a growth mindset, you can transform your habits and transform your life.

Strategies for Habit Formation and Consistency

The ability to form and maintain effective habits is a cornerstone of personal and professional growth. Habits, once ingrained, shape our daily actions, influencing our productivity, well-being, and overall success. This chapter explores a range of strategies designed to facilitate habit formation and cultivate consistency, empowering individuals to transform their aspirations into lasting behavioural changes.

1. Understanding Habit Formation

Before delving into specific strategies, it is crucial to understand the underlying process of habit formation. Habits are formed through repetition and reinforcement, gradually becoming automatic and ingrained in our behaviour. The habit loop, a three-step process, provides a useful framework for understanding this process:

- **Cue:** A trigger or stimulus that initiates the habit.
- **Routine:** The sequence of actions or behaviours that constitute the habit.
- **Reward:** The positive outcome or benefit associated with the habit, reinforcing its repetition.

By understanding the habit loop, individuals can strategically design cues, routines, and rewards to facilitate the formation of new habits and break undesirable ones.

2. Strategies for Habit Formation

2.1 Start Small and Focus on Consistency

One of the most effective strategies for habit formation is to start small and prioritise consistency over intensity. By breaking down large goals into smaller, more manageable actions, individuals can reduce overwhelm and increase the likelihood of success. Focus on performing the desired behaviour consistently, even if it's just for a few minutes each day. This consistent repetition reinforces the habit loop and gradually strengthens the neural pathways associated with the new behaviour.

2.2 Identify Clear Cues and Rewards

Identifying clear cues and rewards is crucial for habit formation. Cues are the triggers that initiate the habit, while rewards provide the positive reinforcement that strengthens the behaviour. Choose cues that are specific, easily recognizable, and consistently present in your environment. Similarly, select rewards that are meaningful and motivating to you, ensuring they are immediate and directly linked to the desired behaviour.

2.3 Design Your Environment

Our environment plays a significant role in shaping our habits. By strategically designing your environment, you can create cues that promote desired behaviours and eliminate triggers that lead to undesirable ones. This can involve rearranging your physical space, removing temptations, or creating visual reminders of your goals.

2.4 Track Your Progress

Tracking your progress is essential for maintaining motivation and staying on track. By monitoring your adherence to your new habit, you can identify patterns, celebrate successes, and address any challenges or setbacks. Utilise tools such as habit trackers, journals, or digital apps to record your progress and visualise your achievements.

2.5 Be Patient and Flexible

Habit formation takes time and effort. It is important to be patient with yourself and allow for flexibility in your approach. There will be days when you falter or miss a step. Don't let these setbacks discourage you. Instead, acknowledge them, learn from them, and recommit to your goal.

3. Strategies for Maintaining Consistency

Once a habit is formed, maintaining consistency is crucial for its long-term sustainability. Here are some strategies to help you stay on track:

- **Set Reminders and Create Routines:** Utilise reminders, such as alarms,

calendar notifications, or visual cues, to prompt yourself to engage in the desired behaviour. Incorporate the habit into your daily routine, creating a consistent pattern that becomes automatic over time.
- **Find an Accountability Partner:** Share your goals with a friend, family member, or colleague who can support and encourage you along the way. Having someone to check in with and share your progress can enhance motivation and accountability.
- **Join a Community or Group:** Connect with others who share similar goals or interests. Participating in a community or group can provide a sense of belonging, support, and inspiration.
- **Celebrate Your Successes:** Acknowledge and celebrate your achievements, no matter how small. Recognizing your progress can reinforce positive behaviours and boost motivation.
- **Review and Adjust Your Strategies:** Regularly review your progress and strategies, making adjustments as needed. If a particular approach is not working, be willing to experiment with new techniques or seek guidance from others.

4. Overcoming Common Challenges

- **Lack of Motivation:** When motivation wanes, remind yourself of the reasons why you started in the first place. Visualise your goals, revisit your initial inspiration, and connect with your deeper purpose.
- **Time Constraints:** If time is a challenge, identify pockets of time in your day where you can incorporate your new habit, even if it's just for a few minutes. Prioritise your goals and eliminate non-essential activities.
- **Setbacks and Relapses:** Setbacks and relapses are a normal part of the habit formation process. Don't let them derail your progress. Acknowledge them, learn from them, and recommit to your goals.
- **Negative Self-Talk:** Challenge negative thoughts and beliefs that can hinder your progress. Replace self-criticism with self-compassion and focus on your strengths and capabilities.
- **Environmental Challenges:** Identify any environmental factors that may be hindering your progress and make adjustments accordingly. This may

involve creating a more conducive environment, removing temptations, or seeking support from others.

5. The Role of Mindset

A growth mindset is essential for successful habit formation and consistency. It involves believing in your ability to learn and grow, embracing challenges, and viewing setbacks as opportunities for learning. Cultivate a positive and optimistic outlook, focusing on your progress rather than perfection.

Habit formation and consistency are key ingredients for achieving excellence. By understanding the process of habit formation, employing effective strategies, and overcoming common challenges, individuals can create lasting behavioural changes that lead to personal and professional growth.

Remember, the journey to excellence is paved with small, consistent steps. Embrace the power of habits, cultivate a growth mindset, and watch as your aspirations transform into reality.

Chapter 9

Mastering Time Management: Optimising Your Workflow for Excellence

Prioritization Techniques and Productivity Hacks

In the relentless pursuit of excellence, time is an invaluable resource. This chapter delves into the art and science of time management, exploring strategies and techniques to optimise your workflow, enhance productivity, and achieve peak performance.

Prioritization Techniques and Productivity Hacks

Effective time management involves more than just creating to-do lists or filling up calendars. It requires a strategic approach to prioritising tasks, eliminating distractions, and maximising efficiency. This section explores various prioritisation techniques and productivity hacks that can empower individuals to achieve more in less time, without sacrificing quality or well-being.

1. The Importance of Prioritization

In today's fast-paced world, we are constantly bombarded with information, demands, and distractions. Without effective prioritisation, it is easy to become overwhelmed and lose focus on what truly matters. Prioritisation allows you to identify the most important tasks, allocate your time and energy efficiently, and make meaningful progress towards your goals.

Benefits of Prioritization:

- **Increased productivity:** By focusing on the most important tasks first, you can accomplish more in less time.
- **Reduced stress:** Prioritisation helps you avoid feeling overwhelmed and stressed by managing your workload effectively.
- **Improved decision-making:** Prioritising tasks forces you to evaluate their importance and urgency, leading to better decision-making.
- **Enhanced focus:** Prioritisation eliminates distractions and allows you to concentrate on the tasks that matter most.

- **Greater sense of accomplishment:** Achieving your most important goals can boost your confidence and motivation.

2. Prioritization Techniques

There are various prioritisation techniques that can help you identify and focus on the most important tasks.

- **The Eisenhower Matrix:** This matrix categorises tasks based on their urgency and importance, helping you prioritise those that are both urgent and important, and delegate or eliminate those that are not.
- **The ABCD Method:** This method involves assigning priorities to tasks based on their importance, with A being the most important and D being the least important.
- **The Ivy Lee Method:** This simple but effective method involves identifying the six most important tasks for the day and prioritising them in order of importance.
- **The Pareto Principle (80/20 Rule):** This principle states that 80% of results come from 20% of efforts. Identify the 20% of

tasks that will yield the greatest results and prioritise them.
- **The MIT (Most Important Tasks) Method:** This method involves identifying the three most important tasks for the day and focusing on completing them before moving on to other tasks.

3. Productivity Hacks

In addition to prioritisation techniques, there are numerous productivity hacks that can help you optimise your workflow and achieve peak performance.

- **Time Blocking:** Allocate specific blocks of time for different tasks or activities, minimising distractions and enhancing focus.
- **Pomodoro Technique:** Break down work into intervals, typically 25 minutes in length, separated by short breaks. This technique can help improve focus and productivity.
- **Batching:** Group similar tasks together and complete them in one go, reducing context switching and improving efficiency.

- **Eliminate Distractions:** Identify and eliminate common distractions, such as social media notifications, email alerts, or unnecessary meetings.
- **Delegate:** Delegate tasks that can be handled by others, freeing up your time to focus on the most important tasks.
- **Automate:** Utilise technology and tools to automate repetitive or time-consuming tasks, increasing efficiency and productivity.
- **Learn to Say No:** Don't overcommit yourself. Learn to say no to requests or tasks that are not aligned with your priorities.
- **Take Breaks:** Regular breaks can help you recharge, improve focus, and prevent burnout.
- **Mindfulness and Meditation:** Practice mindfulness and meditation to reduce stress, improve focus, and enhance overall well-being.
- **Get Enough Sleep:** Adequate sleep is essential for optimal cognitive function, productivity, and overall health.

4. Overcoming Procrastination

Procrastination is a common obstacle to productivity and time management. It involves delaying or postponing tasks, often due to fear, anxiety, or lack of motivation. Here are some strategies to overcome procrastination:

- **Identify the Root Cause:** Understand the underlying reasons for your procrastination, such as fear of failure, perfectionism, or lack of clarity.
- **Break Down Tasks:** Break down large or complex tasks into smaller, more manageable steps, making them seem less daunting.
- **Set Deadlines and Rewards:** Set clear deadlines for tasks and establish rewards for completing them, increasing motivation and accountability.
- **Eliminate Distractions:** Create a distraction-free environment, minimising interruptions and temptations.
- **Use the Two-Minute Rule:** If a task can be completed in two minutes or less, do it immediately.
- **Just Start:** Sometimes the hardest part is getting started. Take the first step, even if it's a small one, and build momentum from there.

- **Seek Support:** If you're struggling with procrastination, don't hesitate to seek support from a friend, colleague, or professional coach.

5. The Role of Technology

Technology can be both a boon and a bane for time management. While it offers numerous tools and apps to enhance productivity, it can also be a source of distraction and overwhelm. Here are some tips for using technology effectively for time management:

- **Choose the Right Tools:** Select tools and apps that align with your needs and workflow, avoiding those that are overly complex or distracting.
- **Set Boundaries:** Establish clear boundaries for technology use, such as turning off notifications during focused work sessions or designating specific times for checking email or social media.
- **Utilise Time-Tracking Apps:** Time-tracking apps can help you monitor how you spend your time and identify areas for improvement.

- **Leverage Automation:** Automate repetitive or time-consuming tasks to free up your time for more important activities.
- **Be Mindful:** Be mindful of how you use technology and avoid letting it consume your time and attention.

Mastering time management is a journey of continuous learning and adaptation. By employing effective prioritisation techniques, productivity hacks, and strategies to overcome procrastination, you can optimise your workflow, enhance your productivity, and achieve peak performance. Remember that time management is not about doing more; it's about doing what matters most. By focusing on the tasks that align with your goals and values, you can achieve excellence in your chosen field and live a more fulfilling and balanced life.

Creating a Sustainable Work-Life Balance

In today's fast-paced and demanding world, achieving a sustainable work-life balance has become an elusive goal for many individuals. The constant pressure to excel in both professional and personal spheres can lead to burnout, stress, and a diminished sense of well-being. This chapter explores the concept of work-life balance, highlighting its importance, and offering strategies for achieving and maintaining a healthy equilibrium between work and personal life.

1. The Importance of Work-Life Balance

Work-life balance refers to the harmonious integration of work and personal life, ensuring that neither aspect dominates or overshadows the other. It involves creating a fulfilling and sustainable lifestyle where individuals can thrive in both their professional and personal roles.

Benefits of Work-Life Balance:

- **Improved Physical and Mental Health:** A healthy work-life balance reduces stress, promotes physical and mental well-being, and decreases the risk of burnout and chronic illnesses.
- **Increased Productivity and Performance:** When individuals feel rested, rejuvenated, and fulfilled in their

personal lives, they tend to be more productive, engaged, and motivated at work.
- **Enhanced Relationships:** A balanced lifestyle allows for quality time with family and friends, fostering strong and supportive relationships.
- **Personal Growth and Development:** Pursuing hobbies, interests, and passions outside of work contributes to personal growth, self-discovery, and a sense of fulfilment.
- **Increased Job Satisfaction:** A healthy work-life balance contributes to greater job satisfaction, as individuals feel more in control of their time and able to pursue both their professional and personal goals.

2. Challenges to Work-Life Balance

Achieving and maintaining a sustainable work-life balance can be challenging in today's demanding work environment. Some common obstacles include:

- **Long working hours and heavy workloads:** The pressure to meet deadlines, achieve targets, and compete in

a global marketplace can lead to long working hours and an excessive workload, leaving little time for personal life.
- **Technology and constant connectivity:** The constant influx of emails, notifications, and work-related messages can blur the boundaries between work and personal life, making it difficult to truly disconnect and recharge.
- **Unrealistic expectations and pressure to perform:** The pressure to constantly perform at a high level, coupled with unrealistic expectations, can create stress and anxiety, making it difficult to achieve a healthy balance.
- **Lack of support and resources:** Individuals may lack the support or resources they need to achieve a work-life balance, such as flexible work arrangements, childcare options, or access to wellness programs.
- **Personal challenges and responsibilities:** Personal challenges, such as caregiving responsibilities or health issues, can further complicate the quest for work-life balance.

3. Strategies for Achieving Work-Life Balance

Achieving a sustainable work-life balance requires intentional effort and a commitment to prioritising both your professional and personal well-being. Here are some effective strategies:

- **Set Boundaries:** Establish clear boundaries between work and personal life. This may involve setting specific work hours, avoiding checking work emails or messages outside of those hours, and creating dedicated time for personal activities and relaxation.
- **Prioritise and Delegate:** Identify your most important tasks and prioritise them accordingly. Delegate tasks that can be handled by others, freeing up your time for more critical activities or personal pursuits.
- **Time Management:** Utilise effective time management techniques, such as creating to-do lists, setting deadlines, and avoiding procrastination, to ensure that you are making the most of your time both at work and in your personal life.

- **Learn to Say No:** Don't overcommit yourself. Learn to say no to additional work or social obligations when you need time for yourself or your loved ones.
- **Take Breaks:** Regular breaks throughout the day can help you recharge, improve focus, and prevent burnout. Step away from your desk, go for a walk, or engage in a relaxing activity to clear your mind and refresh your energy.
- **Mindfulness and Stress Management:** Practise mindfulness techniques, such as meditation or deep breathing exercises, to manage stress and improve overall well-being.
- **Technology Detox:** Regularly disconnect from technology and social media to create space for relaxation, reflection, and meaningful interactions with loved ones.
- **Self-Care:** Prioritise your physical and mental health by getting enough sleep, eating nutritious meals, exercising regularly, and engaging in activities that bring you joy and fulfilment.
- **Communication and Support:** Communicate your needs and boundaries to your employer, colleagues, and loved

ones. Seek support from your network and don't hesitate to ask for help when needed.
- **Flexible Work Arrangements:** Explore flexible work arrangements, such as telecommuting or compressed workweeks, that can allow for greater control over your schedule and a better integration of work and personal life.

4. The Role of Employers

Employers play a crucial role in fostering a culture that supports work-life balance. By implementing policies and practices that promote employee well-being, they can create a more engaged, productive, and loyal workforce. Some effective strategies include:

- **Flexible Work Arrangements:** Offer flexible work arrangements, such as telecommuting, flextime, or compressed workweeks, to accommodate employees' diverse needs and schedules.
- **Wellness Programs:** Provide access to wellness programs, such as gym memberships, stress management workshops, or mental health resources, to

support employees' physical and mental well-being.
- **Family-Friendly Policies:** Implement family-friendly policies, such as paid parental leave, child care assistance, or elder care support, to help employees manage their personal responsibilities.
- **Encouraging Breaks and Vacations:** Encourage employees to take regular breaks and utilise their vacation time to rest, recharge, and pursue personal interests.
- **Setting Realistic Expectations:** Set realistic expectations for workload and deadlines, avoiding excessive pressure and promoting a healthy work environment.
- **Open Communication:** Foster open communication and create a culture where employees feel comfortable discussing their needs and concerns regarding work-life balance.

5. The Importance of Continuous Adaptation

Achieving a sustainable work-life balance is an ongoing process that requires continuous adaptation and adjustment. As your personal and professional circumstances evolve, it is essential to re-evaluate your priorities, strategies, and boundaries to ensure that you are maintaining a healthy equilibrium.

Creating a sustainable work-life balance is not a luxury but a necessity for individuals seeking to thrive in both their professional and personal lives. By setting boundaries, prioritising tasks, managing time effectively, and embracing self-care, individuals can achieve a harmonious integration of work and personal life. Employers also play a vital role in fostering a culture that supports work-life balance, leading to a more engaged, productive, and fulfilled workforce.

Remember, the journey to a sustainable work-life balance is an ongoing process that requires commitment, flexibility, and a willingness to adapt to changing circumstances. By prioritising your well-being and making intentional choices, you can create a fulfilling and balanced lifestyle that allows you to excel in all aspects of your life.

Part IV

Amplifying Your Excellence: Strategies for Visibility and Impact

Chapter 10

The Power of Storytelling: Sharing Your Journey and Inspiring Others

Crafting Compelling Narratives that Resonate

In an era where information overload is commonplace, stories have emerged as a powerful tool for communication, connection, and inspiration. This chapter delves into the art of storytelling, exploring its significance in personal and professional contexts, and providing insights into crafting compelling narratives that resonate with your audience.

Crafting Compelling Narratives that Resonate

Storytelling is more than just recounting events or sharing information. It is about weaving a narrative that captures attention, evokes emotions, and inspires action. Whether you are sharing your personal journey, promoting your brand, or advocating for a cause, the ability to craft compelling narratives can significantly enhance your impact and influence.

1. The Power of Storytelling

Stories have a unique ability to captivate and engage our minds, transcending mere facts and figures. They tap into our emotions, creating a sense of connection and empathy that fosters understanding and inspires action.

- **Engagement and Connection:** Stories create a sense of engagement and connection with the audience, making the information more relatable and memorable.
- **Emotional Impact:** Stories evoke emotions, creating a deeper level of engagement and influencing attitudes and behaviours.
- **Persuasion and Influence:** Stories can be powerful tools for persuasion and influence, as they tap into our values and beliefs.
- **Memorability:** Stories are more likely to be remembered than isolated facts or data,

as they create a narrative structure that is easier for our brains to process and retain.
- **Inspiration and Motivation:** Stories can inspire and motivate, showcasing the possibilities and encouraging others to pursue their dreams.

2. Elements of a Compelling Narrative

A compelling narrative consists of several key elements that work together to create a captivating and impactful story.

- **Characters:** The individuals or entities involved in the story, with whom the audience can identify and empathise.
- **Setting:** The time and place where the story unfolds, providing context and atmosphere.
- **Plot:** The sequence of events that unfold in the story, creating a sense of movement and progression.
- **Conflict:** The challenges or obstacles that the characters face, creating tension and suspense.
- **Resolution:** The way in which the conflict is resolved, providing closure and a sense of satisfaction.

- **Theme:** The underlying message or meaning of the story, often related to universal values or experiences.

3. Crafting Your Narrative

Crafting a compelling narrative involves careful planning and execution. Here are some key steps:

- **Identify Your Purpose:** Clarify the purpose of your story. What message do you want to convey? What action do you want to inspire?
- **Know Your Audience:** Understand your target audience, their interests, values, and pain points. Tailor your story to resonate with them.
- **Develop Your Characters:** Create relatable and engaging characters that your audience can connect with.
- **Create a Compelling Plot:** Craft a plot that is engaging, suspenseful, and emotionally impactful.
- **Use Vivid Language:** Use descriptive language and sensory details to bring your story to life.

- **Incorporate Dialogue:** Dialogue can add depth and realism to your story, making it more engaging.
- **Show, Don't Tell:** Use examples, anecdotes, and metaphors to illustrate your points rather than simply stating them.
- **End with a Strong Conclusion:** Leave a lasting impression on your audience with a memorable and impactful conclusion.

4. Sharing Your Story

Once you have crafted your narrative, it's time to share it with the world. Choose the appropriate channels and platforms to reach your target audience.

- **Written Word:** Share your story through blog posts, articles, or books.
- **Spoken Word:** Deliver your story through presentations, speeches, or podcasts.
- **Visual Storytelling:** Utilise images, videos, or animations to enhance your narrative.

- **Social Media:** Share snippets of your story on social media platforms to engage your audience and build anticipation.
- **Live Events:** Share your story at conferences, workshops, or other live events to connect with your audience in person.

5. The Impact of Storytelling

Storytelling can have a profound impact on individuals and communities. It can:

- **Inspire and Motivate:** Stories of overcoming challenges and achieving success can inspire and motivate others to pursue their dreams.
- **Educate and Inform:** Stories can be used to educate and inform, making complex concepts more accessible and engaging.
- **Build Empathy and Understanding:** Stories can foster empathy and understanding, bridging divides and promoting connection.
- **Create Change:** Stories can be powerful tools for social change, raising awareness and mobilising action.

- **Leave a Legacy:** Stories can preserve memories, pass down traditions, and create a lasting impact on future generations.

The power of storytelling lies in its ability to connect, inspire, and transform. By crafting compelling narratives that resonate with your audience, you can achieve a deeper level of engagement, influence attitudes and behaviours, and create a lasting impact. Whether you are sharing your personal journey, promoting your brand, or advocating for a cause, the art of storytelling can be a powerful tool for achieving your goals and making a difference in the world.

Leveraging Storytelling for Personal Branding

In the digital age, where individuals are constantly vying for attention and recognition, personal branding has become an essential tool for professionals and entrepreneurs alike. While traditional branding focuses on products or services, personal branding centres around the individual, their unique skills, experiences, and values. Storytelling plays a pivotal role in personal branding, allowing individuals to connect with their audience on a deeper level, build trust, and establish a memorable and authentic brand identity.

This section explores the strategies and techniques for leveraging storytelling in personal branding, highlighting its power to differentiate individuals, foster engagement, and create lasting impressions.

1. The Essence of Personal Branding

Personal branding is the process of establishing and promoting your unique identity and value proposition in the professional world. It involves crafting a compelling narrative that showcases your skills, expertise, and personality, and differentiating yourself from others in your field.

Benefits of Personal Branding:

- **Increased Visibility and Recognition:** A strong personal brand can enhance your visibility and recognition in your industry,

making you more memorable and sought-after.
- **Enhanced Credibility and Trust:** By consistently sharing your expertise and insights, you can establish yourself as a thought leader and build trust with your audience.
- **Expanded Network and Opportunities:** A strong personal brand can attract new connections and opportunities, opening doors to collaborations, partnerships, and career advancements.
- **Greater Influence and Impact:** By sharing your story and values, you can inspire and influence others, creating a positive impact in your field and beyond.
- **Career Advancement and Success:** A well-crafted personal brand can accelerate your career progression and open doors to new opportunities.

2. The Role of Storytelling in Personal Branding

Storytelling is a powerful tool for personal branding, as it allows individuals to connect with their audience on an emotional level, build trust, and create a memorable and authentic brand identity.

- **Authenticity and Relatability:** Stories humanise your brand, showcasing your personality, values, and experiences in a way that is relatable and engaging.
- **Emotional Connection:** Stories evoke emotions, creating a deeper level of engagement and fostering a sense of connection with your audience.
- **Memorability:** Stories are more likely to be remembered than facts or figures, as they create a narrative structure that is easier for the brain to process and retain.
- **Differentiation:** Sharing your unique story and experiences can differentiate you from others in your field, highlighting your unique value proposition.
- **Inspiration and Motivation:** Your story can inspire and motivate others, showcasing the possibilities and encouraging them to pursue their own dreams.

3. Crafting Your Personal Brand Story

Crafting a compelling personal brand story involves introspection, reflection, and a deep understanding of your target audience.

- **Identify Your Core Values:** What are the principles that guide your life and work? What do you stand for?
- **Define Your Unique Skills and Expertise:** What are you good at? What sets you apart from others in your field?
- **Highlight Your Accomplishments and Experiences:** What have you achieved? What challenges have you overcome?
- **Showcase Your Personality:** Let your personality shine through in your story. Be authentic and relatable.
- **Connect with Your Audience:** Understand your target audience and tailor your story to resonate with their interests and needs.

4. Sharing Your Story

Once you have crafted your personal brand story, it's time to share it with the world. Utilise various channels and platforms to reach your target audience and amplify your message.

- **Online Presence:** Create a professional website or blog to showcase your story, expertise, and accomplishments.
- **Social Media:** Leverage social media platforms to share snippets of your story, engage with your audience, and build relationships.
- **Content Marketing:** Create valuable content, such as blog posts, articles, videos, or podcasts, that showcase your expertise and provide value to your audience.
- **Public Speaking:** Share your story through presentations, workshops, or conferences, connecting with your audience in person.
- **Networking:** Build relationships with others in your industry and share your story in a genuine and authentic way.

5. Examples of Effective Storytelling in Personal Branding

Numerous individuals have successfully leveraged storytelling to build powerful personal brands.

- **Richard Branson:** The founder of Virgin Group, Richard Branson, often shares stories of his entrepreneurial journey, challenges, and successes, inspiring others to pursue their dreams.
- **Oprah Winfrey:** Oprah Winfrey's personal story of overcoming adversity and achieving success has resonated with millions, establishing her as a powerful and influential figure.
- **Gary Vaynerchuk:** Entrepreneur and social media personality Gary Vaynerchuk uses storytelling to share his insights, experiences, and motivational messages, building a massive following and a strong personal brand.
- **Michelle Obama:** Former First Lady Michelle Obama uses storytelling to connect with audiences, sharing her personal experiences and advocating for causes she believes in.

These examples illustrate the power of storytelling in personal branding, showcasing how individuals can leverage their stories to create a lasting impact and achieve their goals.

In today's competitive landscape, personal branding is essential for professionals and entrepreneurs seeking to stand out and achieve success. Storytelling plays a pivotal role in personal branding, allowing individuals to connect with their audience on a deeper level, build trust, and establish a memorable and authentic brand identity. By crafting a compelling narrative that showcases your unique skills, experiences, and values, and sharing it through various channels and platforms, you can leverage the power of storytelling to enhance your visibility, credibility, and influence, ultimately achieving your personal and professional goals.

Remember that personal branding is an ongoing process that requires consistent effort and authenticity. By staying true to your values, sharing your story with passion, and engaging with your audience, you can build a powerful personal brand that will propel you towards success.

Chapter 11

Building a Strong Online Presence: Connecting with Your Audience

In today's digital age, a robust online presence is essential for individuals and businesses seeking to thrive. The internet and social media platforms have revolutionised the way we connect, communicate, and consume information. This chapter delves into the strategies and tactics for building a strong online presence, emphasising the effective utilisation of social media platforms to engage your audience, build your brand, and achieve your goals.

Utilising Social Media Platforms Effectively

Social media platforms offer a powerful and accessible way to connect with your audience, share your message, and build your brand. However, with the vast array of platforms available and the constant evolution of social media trends, it is essential to approach these platforms strategically and thoughtfully.

1. The Importance of a Strong Online Presence

A strong online presence can significantly impact your personal and professional success. It can:

- **Increase Visibility and Reach:** Expand your reach beyond your immediate network, connecting with potential customers, clients, or collaborators from around the world.
- **Build Brand Awareness and Recognition:** Establish a recognizable and memorable brand identity, fostering trust and credibility.
- **Engage and Connect with Your Audience:** Foster meaningful interactions with your audience, building relationships, and cultivating loyalty.
- **Showcase Your Expertise and Thought Leadership:** Share your knowledge and insights, positioning yourself as an authority in your field.
- **Drive Traffic and Generate Leads:** Attract visitors to your website or landing page, generating leads and potential sales.

- **Enhance Customer Service and Support:** Provide timely and effective customer service through social media channels.
- **Monitor and Manage Your Reputation:** Track mentions of your brand and address any concerns or negative feedback promptly.

2. Choosing the Right Social Media Platforms

With numerous social media platforms available, it is essential to choose the ones that align with your target audience, goals, and brand identity. Consider the following factors:

- **Target Audience:** Identify where your target audience spends their time online and focus your efforts on those platforms.
- **Content Format:** Choose platforms that support the type of content you want to create, whether it's text, images, videos, or a combination.
- **Engagement Style:** Consider the level of interaction and engagement you want to have with your audience and select platforms that facilitate that.

- **Business Goals:** Align your social media strategy with your overall business goals, whether it's brand awareness, lead generation, or customer engagement.

3. Creating Engaging Content

Content is the cornerstone of any successful social media strategy. It is what attracts, engages, and retains your audience. Create content that is:

- **Relevant and Valuable:** Provide content that is relevant to your target audience's interests and needs, offering value and insights.
- **Visually Appealing:** Use high-quality images, videos, and graphics to capture attention and enhance engagement.
- **Consistent with Your Brand:** Maintain a consistent brand voice and visual identity across all your social media content.
- **Shareable and Interactive:** Encourage sharing and interaction by asking questions, running polls, or hosting contests.

- **Optimised for Each Platform:** Tailor your content to the specific requirements and formats of each platform.

4. Building Relationships and Community

Social media is not just about broadcasting your message; it's about building relationships and fostering a sense of community.

- **Engage in Conversations:** Respond to comments, messages, and mentions promptly and thoughtfully.
- **Participate in Relevant Groups and Communities:** Join groups and communities related to your industry or interests to connect with like-minded individuals and share your expertise.
- **Collaborate with Influencers:** Partner with influencers or thought leaders in your field to reach a wider audience and enhance your credibility.
- **Host Live Events or Q&A Sessions:** Interact with your audience in real-time through live events or Q&A sessions, fostering a sense of connection and community.

5. Measuring and Analysing Your Results

Regularly track and analyse your social media metrics to evaluate the effectiveness of your strategy and identify areas for improvement.

- **Key Metrics:** Monitor metrics such as reach, engagement, clicks, conversions, and follower growth.
- **Analytics Tools:** Utilise social media analytics tools to gain insights into your audience demographics, interests, and behaviours.
- **A/B Testing:** Experiment with different content formats, posting times, and calls to action to optimise your results.
- **Adjust and Adapt:** Based on your analysis, adjust your strategy and tactics to improve your performance and achieve your goals.

Building a strong online presence through effective utilisation of social media platforms is essential in today's digital landscape. By choosing the right platforms, creating engaging content, building relationships, and measuring your results, you can connect with your audience, enhance your brand, and achieve your goals. Remember, social media is a dynamic and ever-evolving space. Stay informed about the latest trends, experiment with new strategies, and adapt your approach to stay ahead of the curve and continue to grow your online presence.

Content Marketing Strategies for Audience Engagement

In the digital age, where information is abundant and attention spans are fleeting, captivating and engaging your audience is a paramount challenge. Content marketing, the art of creating and distributing valuable, relevant, and consistent content, has emerged as a powerful tool for achieving this. However, merely producing content is not enough. It is imperative to develop and implement effective strategies that actively engage your audience, fostering a sense of connection, trust, and loyalty. This chapter delves into the world of content marketing strategies, exploring a diverse range of techniques and approaches designed to captivate, resonate, and inspire your target audience.

Understanding Audience Engagement

Before embarking on any content marketing strategy, it is essential to understand the concept of audience engagement. It goes beyond mere views or impressions; it encompasses the level of interaction, connection, and involvement that your audience has with your content. Engaged audiences are more likely to share your content, become loyal customers, and advocate for your brand.

Key indicators of audience engagement:

- **Social Shares:** The number of times your content is shared on social media platforms.
- **Comments and Discussions:** The extent to which your audience interacts with your content through comments, discussions, or questions.
- **Time on Page:** The amount of time visitors spend on your website or blog post.
- **Click-Through Rate (CTR):** The percentage of people who click on a link or call to action within your content.

- **Conversions:** The number of people who take a desired action, such as making a purchase or signing up for a newsletter, after engaging with your content.

Strategies for Audience Engagement

1. Know Your Audience

The foundation of any successful content marketing strategy is a deep understanding of your target audience. Their needs, interests, pain points, and preferences should guide your content creation and distribution efforts. Conduct thorough market research, create detailed buyer personas, and utilise analytics tools to gain insights into your audience's demographics, behaviours, and online habits. By tailoring your content to resonate with your specific audience, you can increase its relevance and engagement potential.

2. Create High-Quality and Valuable Content

The quality of your content is paramount. It should be informative, engaging, and provide genuine value to your audience. Strive to create content that educates, entertains, or inspires, addressing your audience's pain points and offering solutions or insights. Invest in professional content creation, ensuring that your writing, visuals, and overall presentation are polished and compelling. High-quality content not only attracts and engages your audience but also establishes your brand as a credible and trustworthy source of information.

3. Tell Compelling Stories

Storytelling is a powerful tool for capturing attention and forging emotional connections with your audience. Weave narratives into your content that resonate with your audience's values, aspirations, or challenges. Share personal anecdotes, customer success stories, or case studies that illustrate the impact of your products or services. Stories can make your content more memorable, relatable, and shareable, increasing its reach and engagement.

4. Utilise Visuals

Visual content, such as images, videos, infographics, and animations, can significantly enhance engagement. Visuals capture attention, break up text-heavy content, and convey information quickly and effectively. Use high-quality visuals that are relevant to your message and optimised for different platforms and devices. Infographics can present complex data in a visually appealing and easily digestible format, while videos can tell stories, demonstrate products, or provide tutorials in an engaging manner.

5. Encourage Interaction and Participation

Passive consumption of content is not enough to foster engagement. Encourage your audience to actively participate and interact with your content.

- **Ask Questions:** Pose thought-provoking questions at the end of your blog posts, social media updates, or videos to spark conversations and encourage comments.
- **Run Polls and Surveys:** Conduct polls or surveys to gather feedback, insights, and opinions from your audience. This not only provides valuable data but also makes your audience feel heard and valued.
- **Host Contests and Giveaways:** Organise contests or giveaways that require audience participation, such as sharing your content or tagging friends. This can

increase brand awareness, reach, and engagement.
- **Live Events and Webinars:** Host live events, webinars, or Q&A sessions to interact with your audience in real-time, answer questions, and build relationships.

6. Personalise Your Content

Personalization is key to creating a more relevant and engaging experience for your audience. Tailor your content to specific segments of your audience based on their demographics, interests, or behaviours. Utilise data and analytics to gain insights into your audience and create personalised content recommendations, email campaigns, or product offers. Personalization demonstrates that you understand your audience's needs and preferences, fostering a sense of connection and loyalty.

7. Optimise for Search Engines

Search engine optimization (SEO) is crucial for ensuring that your content is discoverable by your target audience. Conduct keyword research to identify the terms and phrases your audience is searching for and incorporate them naturally into your content. Optimise your titles, headings, meta descriptions, and image alt tags to improve your search engine rankings and visibility. By making your content easily accessible to your audience, you increase its reach and engagement potential.

8. Promote Your Content Strategically

Creating great content is only half the battle. Promoting your content strategically is essential for reaching your target audience and maximising its impact.

- **Social Media:** Share your content across relevant social media platforms, utilising eye-catching visuals, compelling headlines, and targeted hashtags.
- **Email Marketing:** Utilise email marketing to deliver your content directly to your subscribers' inboxes, providing them with valuable information and updates.
- **Influencer Marketing:** Partner with influencers or thought leaders in your industry to promote your content and reach a wider audience.

- **Paid Advertising:** Utilise paid advertising platforms, such as Google Ads or social media ads, to target specific demographics or interests and increase your content's visibility.

9. Track, Analyze, and Adapt

Regularly track and analyse your content's performance to gain insights into what resonates with your audience and what doesn't. Utilise analytics tools to monitor metrics such as website traffic, social media engagement, email open rates, and conversion rates. Analyse this data to identify trends, patterns, and areas for improvement. Be willing to adapt your content strategy based on your findings, experimenting with new formats, topics, or distribution channels to optimise your results.

In the digital age, where attention is a precious commodity, content marketing strategies for audience engagement are more important than ever. By understanding your audience, creating high-quality and valuable content, telling compelling stories, utilising visuals, encouraging interaction, personalising your content, optimising for search engines, promoting your content strategically, and tracking your results, you can create a powerful and engaging online presence that resonates with your audience, builds your brand, and achieves your goals. Remember, content marketing is an ongoing process that requires continuous learning, adaptation, and a commitment to providing value to your audience. By prioritising engagement and fostering meaningful connections, you can build a loyal and passionate community that supports your brand and contributes to your long-term success.

Chapter 12

Building a Community of Excellence: Collaboration and Support

The Power of Collaboration and Mentorship
In the pursuit of excellence, individuals and organisations often find themselves navigating a complex and challenging landscape. While individual effort and determination are undoubtedly crucial, the power of collaboration and mentorship cannot be underestimated.

This chapter delves into the profound impact of building a community of excellence, exploring the benefits of collaboration, the transformative role of mentorship, and the strategies for fostering a supportive and empowering environment where individuals can thrive and achieve their full potential.

The Power of Collaboration and Mentorship

Collaboration and mentorship are two pillars that underpin the foundation of a thriving community of excellence. Collaboration fosters synergy, innovation, and collective growth, while mentorship provides guidance, support, and inspiration. By harnessing the power of these two forces, individuals and organisations can create an environment where excellence flourishes.

1. The Benefits of Collaboration

Collaboration is the act of working together with others to achieve a common goal. It involves sharing ideas, resources, and expertise, and leveraging the collective strengths of a team or community to achieve greater outcomes.

- **Synergy and Innovation:** Collaboration brings together diverse perspectives and skillsets, fostering synergy and sparking innovation. By combining their unique strengths, individuals can generate new ideas, solve complex problems, and achieve breakthroughs that would not be possible alone.
- **Collective Growth and Learning:** Collaboration provides opportunities for

shared learning and growth. By working alongside others, individuals can gain new insights, develop new skills, and expand their knowledge base.
- **Increased Efficiency and Productivity:** Collaboration can streamline processes, optimise workflows, and leverage shared resources, leading to increased efficiency and productivity.
- **Enhanced Problem-Solving:** By pooling their collective wisdom and experience, teams can tackle challenges more effectively and develop creative solutions.
- **Stronger Relationships and Networks:** Collaboration fosters connections and builds relationships, creating a supportive and empowering network where individuals can thrive.

2. The Transformative Role of Mentorship

Mentorship is a relationship between a more experienced or knowledgeable individual (the mentor) and a less experienced individual (the mentee). The mentor provides guidance, support, and encouragement to the mentee, helping them navigate challenges, develop their skills, and achieve their goals.

- **Guidance and Support:** Mentors offer valuable guidance and support, sharing their knowledge, experience, and insights to help mentees navigate their journey towards excellence.
- **Inspiration and Motivation:** Mentors can serve as role models, inspiring and motivating mentees to reach their full potential.
- **Skill Development:** Mentors can help mentees develop specific skills and competencies, providing feedback, coaching, and opportunities for practice.
- **Career Advancement:** Mentors can offer advice and guidance on career paths, networking, and professional development, helping mentees achieve their career goals.
- **Personal Growth:** Mentorship can also foster personal growth, helping mentees develop self-awareness, confidence, and resilience.

3. Strategies for Fostering Collaboration

Creating a collaborative environment requires intentional effort and a commitment to fostering open communication, trust, and mutual respect.

Here are some strategies to promote collaboration:

- **Open Communication:** Encourage open and honest communication, creating a safe space for individuals to share ideas, concerns, and feedback.
- **Shared Goals and Vision:** Establish clear and shared goals, ensuring everyone understands the collective purpose and works towards a common vision.
- **Team Building:** Invest in team-building activities and initiatives to foster trust, camaraderie, and a sense of belonging among team members.
- **Empowerment and Autonomy:** Empower individuals to take ownership of their work, make decisions, and contribute their unique perspectives.
- **Recognition and Appreciation:** Acknowledge and appreciate the contributions of individuals and teams, fostering a culture of recognition and gratitude.
- **Conflict Resolution:** Develop effective conflict resolution strategies to address disagreements and maintain a positive and collaborative environment.

4. Strategies for Cultivating Mentorship

Cultivating mentorship involves creating opportunities for meaningful connections and fostering relationships that support growth and development. Here are some strategies to promote mentorship:

- **Formal Mentorship Programs:** Establish formal mentorship programs that match mentors and mentees based on their skills, interests, and goals.
- **Informal Mentorship Opportunities:** Encourage informal mentorship relationships to develop organically within the organisation, fostering a culture of learning and support.
- **Mentorship Training and Resources:** Provide training and resources to mentors and mentees, equipping them with the skills and knowledge to build effective mentorship relationships.
- **Mentorship Recognition and Rewards:** Acknowledge and reward mentors for their contributions, recognizing their commitment to supporting the growth and development of others.

- **Mentorship Evaluation and Feedback:** Regularly evaluate the effectiveness of mentorship programs and seek feedback from mentors and mentees to identify areas for improvement.

5. Overcoming Challenges

Building a community of excellence through collaboration and mentorship is not without its challenges. Here are some common obstacles and strategies to overcome them:

- **Competition and Ego:** In some cases, competition and ego can hinder collaboration and create a culture of individualism. Foster a collaborative mindset by emphasising shared goals, recognizing collective achievements, and promoting a culture of mutual support.
- **Lack of Trust:** Trust is essential for effective collaboration and mentorship. Build trust by promoting transparency, open communication, and demonstrating respect for diverse perspectives.
- **Time Constraints:** Busy schedules and competing priorities can make it challenging to dedicate time to

collaboration and mentorship. Encourage individuals to prioritise these activities, recognizing their long-term benefits for both personal and organisational growth.
- **Mismatched Mentorship Pairings:** Not all mentorship relationships are successful. Ensure that mentors and mentees are well-matched based on their skills, interests, and goals, and provide ongoing support and guidance to both parties.

Building a community of excellence requires a commitment to collaboration, mentorship, and fostering a supportive and empowering environment. By harnessing the power of collective wisdom, shared learning, and guidance from experienced individuals, individuals and organisations can unlock their full potential, overcome challenges, and achieve remarkable success. Remember, excellence is not a solo pursuit; it is a collective endeavour that thrives in a community where collaboration and mentorship are valued and nurtured.

Fostering a Supportive Network for Continuous Growth

In the pursuit of excellence, the journey is rarely a solitary one. Individuals and organisations alike thrive within a supportive network that fosters continuous growth, providing encouragement, resources, and opportunities for development. This chapter delves into the profound impact of building and nurturing a supportive network, exploring its role in personal and professional development, and highlighting strategies for creating a thriving ecosystem where individuals can flourish and achieve their full potential.

1. The Importance of a Supportive Network

A supportive network encompasses a web of connections and relationships that provide individuals and organisations with the resources, encouragement, and opportunities they need to grow and succeed. It can include mentors, colleagues, friends, family members, professional organisations, and online communities.

Benefits of a Supportive Network:

- **Emotional Support:** A supportive network provides a safe space for individuals to share their challenges, receive encouragement, and feel validated in their struggles and triumphs.
- **Knowledge and Expertise:** A network of diverse individuals can offer a wealth of knowledge, expertise, and perspectives, facilitating learning and growth.
- **Collaboration and Opportunities:** A supportive network can open doors to new opportunities, collaborations, and partnerships, expanding horizons and fostering innovation.
- **Accountability and Motivation:** A network of peers and mentors can provide accountability, motivation, and encouragement, helping individuals stay on track and achieve their goals.
- **Sense of Belonging and Community:** A supportive network creates a sense of belonging and community, fostering a positive and empowering environment where individuals feel connected and valued.

2. Building a Supportive Network

Building a supportive network requires intentionality, proactivity, and a genuine desire to connect with others. It involves stepping outside your comfort zone, initiating conversations, and nurturing relationships over time.

2.1 Identifying Key Connections

Begin by identifying individuals who can contribute to your growth and development. These can include:

- **Mentors:** Experienced individuals who can offer guidance, advice, and support based on their own experiences and expertise.
- **Peers:** Colleagues or individuals in your field who can share insights, collaborate on projects, and provide mutual support.
- **Industry Leaders:** Thought leaders and influencers in your industry who can provide inspiration, knowledge, and access to new opportunities.
- **Friends and Family:** Loved ones who can offer emotional support, encouragement, and a safe space to share your challenges and successes.

- **Online Communities:** Virtual communities and forums related to your interests or field can provide a platform for connecting with like-minded individuals, sharing knowledge, and accessing resources.

2.2 Cultivating Relationships

Once you have identified key connections, it is essential to cultivate and nurture these relationships over time. This involves:

- **Active Communication:** Engage in regular communication, whether through in-person meetings, phone calls, emails, or virtual interactions.
- **Genuine Interest:** Show genuine interest in others, their work, and their goals. Actively listen and offer support and encouragement.
- **Reciprocity:** Be willing to give as much as you receive. Offer your own expertise, insights, and support to others in your network.
- **Shared Values:** Seek out individuals who share your values and aspirations. This

can create a strong foundation for meaningful and lasting connections.
- **Appreciation and Gratitude:** Express appreciation and gratitude for the support and contributions of others in your network.

3. Strategies for Fostering a Supportive Environment

Creating a supportive environment within your network involves cultivating a culture of trust, respect, and mutual empowerment. Here are some strategies to foster such an environment:

- **Open Communication:** Encourage open and honest communication, creating a safe space for individuals to share their ideas, concerns, and feedback.
- **Active Listening:** Practise active listening, demonstrating genuine interest in others' perspectives and experiences.
- **Constructive Feedback:** Provide constructive feedback that is specific, actionable, and focused on growth and development.

- **Collaboration and Shared Learning:** Encourage collaboration and knowledge-sharing among members of your network.
- **Celebration and Recognition:** Acknowledge and celebrate the achievements and milestones of others in your network, fostering a sense of shared success.
- **Empathy and Support:** Offer empathy and support to others during challenging times, demonstrating compassion and understanding.
- **Diversity and Inclusion:** Embrace diversity and create an inclusive environment where everyone feels valued and respected.

4. Overcoming Challenges

Building and maintaining a supportive network can encounter challenges. Here are some common obstacles and strategies to overcome them:

- **Time Constraints:** Busy schedules and competing priorities can make it challenging to dedicate time to networking and relationship building.

Prioritise networking activities, even if it's just for a few minutes each day, and leverage technology to connect with others virtually.

- **Limited Resources:** Access to mentors, industry leaders, or professional development opportunities may be limited. Seek out free or low-cost resources, such as online communities, webinars, or workshops, and leverage your existing network to connect with potential mentors.
- **Fear of Rejection:** Fear of rejection or self-doubt can prevent individuals from reaching out and building new connections. Challenge these negative thoughts, focus on your strengths, and remember that everyone starts somewhere.
- **Maintaining Relationships:** Nurturing relationships requires ongoing effort and attention. Make time for regular communication, express appreciation, and offer support to others in your network.

5. The Role of Technology

Technology has transformed the way we connect and build relationships, offering new opportunities for creating and nurturing supportive networks.

- **Social Media:** Leverage social media platforms to connect with individuals in your field, share your expertise, and engage in meaningful conversations.
- **Online Communities:** Participate in online communities and forums related to your interests or field to connect with like-minded individuals, access resources, and share knowledge.
- **Virtual Events:** Attend virtual conferences, webinars, or workshops to expand your network, learn from experts, and gain new insights.
- **Mentorship Platforms:** Utilise online mentorship platforms to connect with experienced individuals who can offer guidance and support.

Fostering a supportive network is essential for personal and professional growth. By building meaningful connections, cultivating relationships, and creating a supportive environment, individuals and organisations can access valuable resources, encouragement, and opportunities for development. Embrace the power of collaboration, seek out mentors, and actively participate in your network to unlock your full potential and achieve excellence in your chosen field. Remember, the journey to success is not a solo endeavour; it is a collective journey that thrives within a supportive and empowering community.

CONCLUSION

Throughout this exploration of excellence, we have traversed a landscape of principles, strategies, and insights designed to empower individuals and organisations to reach their full potential. We have delved into the power of purpose, the importance of differentiation, the cultivation of effective habits, the mastery of time management, the embrace of a growth mindset, the resilience in overcoming challenges, the art of storytelling, and the significance of building a supportive network. While each chapter has offered valuable lessons and actionable steps, the pursuit of excellence is not a destination but a lifelong journey.

Maintaining Momentum and Avoiding Stagnation

The journey toward excellence is marked by continuous progress and growth. It is essential to maintain momentum and avoid stagnation, even after achieving significant milestones. Complacency can be a formidable foe, lulling individuals and organisations into a false sense of security and hindering further development.

To maintain momentum, embrace a mindset of continuous learning and improvement. Seek out new challenges, expand your knowledge and skills, and stay abreast of industry trends. Foster a culture of innovation and experimentation, encouraging creativity and risk-taking. Celebrate successes, but don't rest on your laurels. Instead, use them as stepping stones to even greater achievements.

Embracing Continuous Learning and Growth

In a rapidly changing world, continuous learning and growth are essential for staying relevant and competitive. Embrace a growth mindset, believing in your ability to learn and evolve. Seek out new knowledge, skills, and experiences, both within and outside your field of expertise.

- **Read Widely:** Read books, articles, and blogs on a variety of topics to expand your knowledge and perspectives.
- **Take Courses and Workshops:** Enrol in courses or workshops to learn new skills or deepen your understanding of a particular subject.

- **Seek Mentorship:** Find mentors who can offer guidance, support, and insights based on their own experiences.
- **Network with Others:** Connect with individuals in your field and beyond to exchange ideas, collaborate on projects, and learn from their experiences.
- **Reflect on Your Experiences:** Take time to reflect on your successes and failures, identifying lessons learned and areas for improvement.

The Ripple Effect: Inspiring Excellence in Others

As you progress on your journey towards excellence, remember that your actions and achievements can have a ripple effect, inspiring and motivating others to pursue their own goals. Share your knowledge, experiences, and insights with others, offering guidance and support to those who are just starting their journey.

- **Mentorship:** Become a mentor to others, sharing your wisdom and expertise to help them grow and develop.
- **Collaboration:** Collaborate with others on projects and initiatives, fostering a

culture of shared learning and collective achievement.
- **Lead by Example:** Set a positive example through your own actions and behaviours, demonstrating the values and habits that contribute to excellence.
- **Share Your Story:** Share your journey and the lessons you've learned along the way, inspiring others to overcome challenges and pursue their dreams.
- **Give Back to Your Community:** Contribute your time and resources to support causes you believe in, making a positive impact on the world around you.

The Journey Continues

The pursuit of excellence is a lifelong journey, marked by continuous learning, growth, and adaptation. Embrace the challenges, celebrate the successes, and never stop striving to reach your full potential. Remember, excellence is not about perfection; it's about progress, perseverance, and a relentless pursuit of your goals.

As you continue on your journey, remember the key principles and strategies we have explored:

- **Purpose:** Align your goals with a higher purpose, creating a sense of meaning and motivation.
- **Differentiation:** Identify and leverage your unique strengths and value proposition to stand out from the crowd.
- **Habits:** Cultivate effective habits that support your goals and contribute to your overall well-being.
- **Time Management:** Master time management techniques to optimise your workflow and achieve peak performance.
- **Growth Mindset:** Embrace a growth mindset, believing in your ability to learn and evolve.
- **Resilience:** Develop resilience to overcome challenges and setbacks, emerging stronger and more determined.
- **Storytelling:** Leverage the power of storytelling to connect with others, share your journey, and inspire action.
- **Community:** Build a supportive network of mentors, peers, and colleagues to foster collaboration, learning, and growth.

By integrating these principles into your life and work, you can create a fulfilling and impactful journey towards excellence, leaving a lasting legacy for yourself and those around you.

Final Thoughts

The pursuit of excellence is not a destination; it is a way of life. It is a continuous process of learning, growth, and adaptation, fueled by passion, purpose, and a relentless pursuit of your goals. Embrace the challenges, celebrate the successes, and never stop striving to reach your full potential. Remember, the journey is just as important as the destination. So, enjoy the ride, embrace the lessons, and continue to inspire excellence in yourself and others. The world is waiting for your unique contributions.

Appendix

Resources for Further Exploration

The pursuit of excellence is a lifelong journey, and the resources listed below can provide further guidance, inspiration, and support as you continue to grow and develop. These resources include books, articles, websites, podcasts, and other tools that can help you deepen your understanding of the concepts and strategies discussed in this book, and apply them to your own life and work.

Books:

- **Mindset: The New Psychology of Success** by Carol S. Dweck: This groundbreaking book explores the power of mindset and how it can impact our lives. Dweck explains the difference between a fixed mindset and a growth mindset, and how embracing a growth mindset can lead to greater success and fulfilment.
- **Atomic Habits: An Easy & Proven Way to Build Good Habits & Break Bad Ones** by James Clear: This practical guide

provides a step-by-step framework for building good habits and breaking bad ones. Clear explains the science behind habit formation and offers actionable strategies for creating lasting change.
- **Drive: The Surprising Truth About What Motivates Us** by Daniel H. Pink: This insightful book explores the science of motivation, challenging traditional reward-and-punishment systems and highlighting the importance of intrinsic motivation. Pink offers strategies for fostering autonomy, mastery, and purpose in both personal and professional settings.
- **The 7 Habits of Highly Effective People** by Stephen R. Covey: This classic self-help book outlines seven habits that can lead to personal and professional effectiveness. Covey's principles of proactivity, prioritisation, and synergy continue to resonate with readers decades after its publication.
- **Daring Greatly: How the Courage to Be Vulnerable Transforms the Way We Live, Love, Parent, and Lead** by Brené Brown: This powerful book explores the importance of vulnerability and courage in our lives. Brown challenges the notion

that vulnerability is a weakness and shows how embracing it can lead to greater connection, creativity, and resilience.
- **The Power of Habit: Why We Do What We Do in Life and Business** by Charles Duhigg: This fascinating book explores the science behind habits, explaining how they are formed and how they can be changed. Duhigg offers insights into how habits shape our lives and how we can harness their power to achieve our goals.
- **Start with Why: How Great Leaders Inspire Everyone to Take Action** by Simon Sinek: This influential book challenges leaders to start with why, focusing on their purpose and beliefs rather than just what they do or how they do it. Sinek argues that inspiring leaders communicate their why, creating a sense of connection and loyalty among their followers.

Articles:

- **"The Power of a Growth Mindset"** by Carol S. Dweck: This article provides a concise overview of the growth mindset and its benefits. Dweck explains how

embracing a growth mindset can lead to greater resilience, learning, and achievement.
- **"How to Build Better Habits"** by James Clear: This article offers practical tips for building good habits and breaking bad ones. Clear emphasises the importance of starting small, focusing on consistency, and creating a supportive environment.
- **"The Surprising Science of Motivation"** by Daniel H. Pink: This article summarises the key findings from Pink's book "Drive," highlighting the importance of intrinsic motivation and offering strategies for fostering autonomy, mastery, and purpose.
- **"The 7 Habits of Highly Effective People: Powerful Lessons in Personal Change"** by Stephen R. Covey: This article revisits Covey's seven habits, providing a refresher on their significance and offering insights into how they can be applied in today's world.
- **"The Power of Vulnerability"** by Brené Brown: This article explores the concept of vulnerability and its role in building connection, fostering creativity, and living a wholehearted life.

- **"The Habits That Shape Our Lives"** by Charles Duhigg: This article provides a summary of Duhigg's book "The Power of Habit," explaining the science behind habits and offering strategies for changing them.
- **"Start With Why: How Great Leaders Inspire Action"** by Simon Sinek: This article outlines Sinek's concept of starting with why, emphasising the importance of purpose and belief in leadership and communication.

Websites:

- **Mindset Works:** This website offers resources and tools for developing a growth mindset, including articles, videos, and activities.
- **James Clear:** This website features a wealth of articles, videos, and tools on habit formation, productivity, and personal development.
- **Daniel H. Pink:** This website provides information about Pink's books, articles, and speaking engagements, as well as resources on motivation and engagement.

- **The 7 Habits of Highly Effective People:** This website offers resources and tools for applying Covey's seven habits, including workshops, training programs, and online courses.
- **Brené Brown:** This website features information about Brown's research, books, and speaking engagements, as well as resources on vulnerability, courage, and wholehearted living.
- **Charles Duhigg:** This website provides information about Duhigg's books, articles, and speaking engagements, as well as resources on habits and behaviour change.
- **Simon Sinek:** This website features information about Sinek's books, articles, and speaking engagements, as well as resources on leadership and communication.

Podcasts:

- **The Mindset Mentor:** This podcast features interviews with experts and thought leaders on mindset, motivation, and personal development.

- **The James Clear Podcast:** This podcast explores topics related to habit formation, productivity, and personal growth, featuring interviews with experts and insights from Clear's own research and experience.
- **The Daniel H. Pink Podcast:** This podcast features conversations with Pink and other experts on motivation, engagement, and the future of work.
- **The 7 Habits Podcast:** This podcast explores the principles of Covey's seven habits and offers practical tips for applying them in your life.
- **Unlocking Us with Brené Brown:** This podcast features conversations with Brown and other guests on topics related to vulnerability, courage, and wholehearted living.
- **Hidden Brain:** This podcast explores the unconscious patterns that drive human behaviour, offering insights into habits, decision-making, and social interactions.
- **TED Radio Hour:** This podcast features TED Talks on a variety of topics, including science, technology, and personal development.

Other Tools and Resources:

- **Habit trackers:** Habit trackers can help you monitor your progress and stay accountable to your goals.
- **Journaling:** Journaling can be a powerful tool for self-reflection, goal setting, and tracking your progress.
- **Meditation and mindfulness practices:** Meditation and mindfulness practices can help you reduce stress, improve focus, and cultivate a positive mindset.
- **Coaching and mentoring:** A coach or mentor can provide personalised guidance and support as you work towards your goals.
- **Online communities and forums:** Connect with like-minded individuals online to share ideas, exchange knowledge, and find support.

The pursuit of excellence is an ongoing journey, and the resources listed above can provide valuable guidance and support as you continue to grow and develop. Remember, the key is to be proactive, intentional, and persistent in your efforts. By embracing a growth mindset, cultivating effective habits, and surrounding yourself with a supportive network, you can achieve remarkable results and live a fulfilling and impactful life.

Index

- **A**
    - Accountability
    - Action Plans
        - Creating
        - Importance of
    - Actionable Steps
        - Benefits of
        - Key Considerations for Developing
    - Active Engagement
    - Active Learning Strategies
    - Adaptability
    - Aspirations
        - Power of
        - Setting Aspirational Goals
    - Authenticity
    - Automation
- **B**
    - Batching

- Benchmarking
- Brand Experience
- Brand Identity
- Brand Story
- Building a Supportive Network
- Burnout

- **C**
  - Challenges
    - Common
    - External
    - Internal
    - Nature of
    - Overcoming
    - Strategies for Overcoming
  - Collaboration
    - Benefits of
    - Strategies for Fostering
  - Communication
  - Community of Excellence
  - Competitive Advantage
  - Consistency
    - Strategies for Maintaining
  - Continuous Improvement
    - Culture of

- **D**
  - Delegation
  - Differentiation

www.ingramcontent.com/pod-product-compliance
Lightning Source LLC
Chambersburg PA
CBHW052148220526
45471CB00004B/1582